THE LIBERATING MISSION OF JESUS

Pentecostals, Peacemaking, and Social Justice Series

PAUL ALEXANDER AND JAY BEAMAN, SERIES EDITORS

Volumes in the Series:

Pentecostal Pacifism: The Origin, Development, and Rejection of Pacific Belief among the Pentecostals
by Jay Beaman

A Liberating Spirit: Pentecostals and Social Action in North America
edited by Michael Wilkinson and Steven M. Studebaker

Forgiveness, Reconciliation, and Restoration: Multidisciplinary Studies from a Pentecostal Perspective
edited by Martin W. Mittelstadt and Geoffrey W. Sutton

Christ at the Checkpoint: Theology in the Service of Justice and Peace
edited by Paul Alexander

Pentecostals and Nonviolence: Reclaiming a Heritage
edited by Paul Alexander

The Liberating Mission of Jesus

The Message of the Gospel of Luke

Darío López Rodriguez

TRANSLATED FROM THE SPANISH BY

STEFANIE D. ISRAEL

FOREWORD BY

SAMUEL ESCOBAR

PICKWICK *Publications* · Eugene, Oregon

THE LIBERATING MISSION OF JESUS
Pentecostals, Peacemaking, and Social Justice 6

Pickwick Publications
An Imprint of Wipf and Stock Publishers
199 W. 8th Ave., Suite 3
Eugene, OR 97401

www.wipfandstock.com

ISBN 13: 978-1-61097-516-2

Cataloging-in-Publication data:

Rodriguez, Darío López.

    [La mision liberadora de Jesus : el mensaje del evangelio de Lucas.
    The liberating mission of Jesus / Darío López Rodriguez ; foreword by Samuel Escobar; translated by Stephanie D. Israel. English]

    xvi + 142 p. ; 23 cm. —Includes bibliographical references.

    Pentecostals, Peacemaking, and Social Justice 6

    ISBN 13: 978-1-61097-516-2

    1. Bible. N.T. Luke—Criticism, interpretation, etc. 2. Liberation theology—Latin America. 3. Church and social problems—Latin America. 4. Pentecostalism—Peru. I. Escobar, Samuel. II. Israel, Stephanie D. III. Title. IV. Series.

BS2595.52 .L67 2012

Originally published as *La Misión Liberadora de Jesús: El Mensaje del Evangelio de Lucas* © 1997 Ediciones Puma. Translated from the second Spanish edition, © 2004 Ediciones Puma.

To Mount Sinai Church of God in Peru, a Pentecostal congregation in which I met and learned to love the God of life. To the Pentecostal women who, inserted in the survival organizations, fight day by day against poverty, through this giving testimony of their unconquerable commitment to the God of life. To them I express my gratitude and pay homage.

Contents

Foreword

That a biblical studies book written in Latin America should reach its second edition is an editorial happening worthy of celebration. For this reason, I have accepted the invitation to write these lines, in a celebratory attitude in support of the author, who I have the privilege to know as a friend and colleague. I believe that this exegetical and pastoral work unites academic quality with a special virtue sprouting out of the Christian practice of its author as a pastor and teacher.

Dr. Darío López is known in Peru and Latin America for his work as an organizer of student communities, as pastor of a church on the outskirts of Lima, as an active participant in the efforts of the National Evangelical Council of Peru (CONEP), of which he was president, and in the fight against corruption and in favor of human rights in marginalized sectors of Peruvian society. Various books written by Dr. López testify to his militant effort to interpret the reality of the Latin American Pentecostal movement from within. Yet, this book on the gospel of Luke shows us the spirituality that nourishes the ministerial and civic actions of its author. In its pages, we draw near to the intimacy of the author's relationship with Christ and his effort to articulate the evangelical faith as a reflection on his own practice as someone who listens to the Lord of life, devotes himself to a life of obedience to the call of Jesus, and reflects in light of the Word of God.

I have used this book as a study text in my teaching in the Americas and Europe, especially in courses dedicated to the foundations and understanding of Christian mission in the twenty-first century. An important reference point for men and women that approach the text of

Luke today is that the author of this work is not a classroom academic, but a Pentecostal pastor that lives on the frontiers of service to the poor. This second edition has been enriched with new chapters, and at various points the author has corrected and refined his treatment of the biblical text, also updating references to bibliographical sources. All of this will be of great help to scholars who wish to deepen their understanding of the third gospel, beginning with the missiological and pastoral fundamentals that Dr. López offers us with such clarity.

Reading the text of the evangelist Luke with questions that emerge from current missionary practice means reading it with an intention much closer to that of Luke, the first historian of Christian mission. This book enters into dialogue with the strictly missiological approaches of scholars like David Bosch, Orlando Costas, and René Padilla. Whoever ministers among the poor is also unable to avoid dialoguing with authors like Gustavo Gutiérrez, the well-known liberation theologian, whose work of various decades has accumulated a wealth of readings of the biblical text to which reference is required. However, Darío López cannot be said to be a liberation theologian, as it becomes clear to whoever attentively reads this work that its author is fundamentally an evangelical pastor. The questions of the text come from his pastoral practice and his sources reflect respect for the authority of the biblical text and consciousness of the illuminating work of the Holy Spirit, in accordance with the best practices of evangelical tradition.

We live in a confusing time in which many evangelical publishers flood us with texts from popular North American authors, which are superficial and completely outside of our reality, but are imposed upon us by their publicity efforts. For this reason, I greet with special joy the appearance of the second edition of this valuable work by a Peruvian pastor and scholar, thanks to the work and enthusiasm of a Peruvian publishing house. May God continue to use this book for the edification of his people and as a testimony to a world in need of light and hope.

Samuel Escobar
Valencia (Spain), April 2004

Prologue to the First Spanish Edition

One of the reasons that has compelled me to study the Lucan perspective on mission more frequently in recent years is the close relationship that Jesus of Nazareth had with the fragile members of the Judean society of his time, the poor and excluded (tax-collectors, lepers, Samaritans, women, the sick, and children), a theme that presents itself as a distinguishing characteristic of the third gospel. The special love of God for the dispossessed and disinherited and the universality of mission are two theological foci of Luke that indicate both the commitment that evangelical churches need to make at all times and the path that they need to follow in every historical context. Understanding the message of Luke's gospel, the way Jesus treated and valued the needy and the destitute, has been of great help in my pastoral work in one of the marginal urban neighborhoods in the southern part of Lima, Peru (Villa María del Triunfo). As this book of the New Testament highlights the unfathomable value of life, a principle of the good news of the kingdom of God, may it call into question dehumanizing religious practices and cultural patterns that objectify human beings created in the image of God.

According to Luke, during Jesus' missionary journeys through cities and villages, he constantly connected with those who were of the lowest social rank and confined to social ostracism. This explains why, from the Lucan theological perspective, the liberating mission of Jesus—centered around the proclamation of the good news of the kingdom of God through word and concrete action—expresses itself visibly in the close relationship that exists between the following elements that form the unbreakable chain of self-giving love: going, seeing, compassion, commitment, and transformation.[1]

This relationship that summarizes the liberating mission of Jesus is more than a list of optional guidelines for action or simple hermeneutical guidelines disconnected from one another. Rather, it establishes an integral program for the defense of life and human dignity, a task which evangelical churches cannot evade.

The different chapters of this book seek to explain and expand on the concrete reach of the principles for mission mentioned above. Each one deals with a specific theme related to the Lucan emphasis on the special love that God has for the poor and defenseless of the world. My reading of the Lucan testimony revolves around this key theme, in light of the universality of mission and the universal reach of salvation. Furthermore, each chapter attempts to connect biblical theology with the particular ethical challenges of our mission field.

The themes dealt with here were first shared in the worship services and leaders meetings at Mount Sinai Church of God, a Pentecostal congregation located in the Villa María del Triunfo district of Lima, Peru. The communal times of Bible study and conversations with local church members were incredibly useful in deepening the study of texts deliberately chosen to address questions about the mission of the church that daily presented themselves as recurring issues in pastoral work. The first chapter was written for a conference on Biblical Perspectives of Mission, organized by Dr. C. René Padilla in October of 1995. This chapter forms part of the book *Bases Bíblicas de la Misión* (Biblical Foundations for Mission), edited by C. René Padilla. It has also been published in the magazine *Transformation* (vol. 14, no. 3, 1997). The second chapter is a revised version of a section of my master's thesis that I presented at *Facultad Evangélica Orlando Costas* (Orlando Costas Evangelical College) in Lima in 1993.[2] The other chapters are previously unpublished. Some of them circulated as documents that were used in meetings with students of the Association of Evangelical University Groups of Peru (1995 and 1996), in the devotionals of Compassion International—Peru (1997), and

1 René Padilla, when referring to what he calls the chain of self-giving love, specifies that this chain has three principles: seeing, having compassion, and acting ("Ser Prójimo," 148). Guillermo Cook prefers to use the trinomial: seeing, judging, and acting ("Ver, Juzgar y Actuar," 96).

2. *Misión, Pobreza, y Marginalidad: Una Lectura Contextual del Evangelio de Lucas* (Mission, Poverty, and Marginality: A Contextual Reading of Luke's Gospel).

in the first Human Rights Encounter organized by the Church of God in Peru (1997).

These works, which have been incubating over the past six years, appear here in the form of a book, with the sole purpose of dialoging publicly with all those who are committed to the mission of God in distinct social, political, and cultural frontiers. Particularly, I believe that if dialogue is better than monologue and collective work is healthier than individual prominence, then it will always be useful and necessary to mutually give feedback on the path of service to the Lord of mission. It is my prayer that the following reflections contribute to the achievement of this purpose.

Darío López Rodríguez
Villa María del Triunfo, December 1997

Prologue to the Second Spanish Edition

All books have a history. But certain books develop and are constructed from particular experiences and concrete commitments to a greater cause. I do not deny, for it would be improper and dishonest to do so, that this book was developed within a concrete reality of misery and oppression. For this reason, its reading of Luke's gospel can seem uncomfortable for evangelical Christians who dare not come face-to-face with the contemptible situation of extreme material poverty that millions of human beings of flesh and bone find themselves in, among them thousands of believers. But Luke is the gospel for the exiled of the earth, for the outcasts that make up the "human refuse" that the invisible hand of the market abusively coughs up, for the destitute and needy of the world that have the God of life as their *go'el*. Indeed, according to the testimony of the third gospel, God has a special love for all those who have been condemned to social ostracism and the basement of history by those who hold political and economic power. Luke emphasizes that a real goal of the liberating mission of Jesus is to reverse the destiny of the poor and the excluded. The Lucan Jesus stands up for the destitute and dispossessed, includes the excluded, socially reinserts the outcasts, humanizes that which society objectifies, and dignifies those who are the social waste of the powerful.

This book, which by the grace of God is already in its second edition, attempts to explain the message of the third gospel and proposes that at the heart of the liberating mission of Jesus are two non-negotiable themes: the universality of mission and the special love of God of the poor and the excluded. These two pillars, upon which the Lucan theological proposition rests, are present in the biblical story, told only in Luke, known as the programmatic discourse of Nazareth or the messianic manifesto of Nazareth. Luke 4:16–30—a key text that is undeniably connected to the concept of the Jubilee and has precise social and political connotations— summarizes the whole gospel in the same way that Acts 1:8 summarizes the book of Acts.

The second edition of this book contains new chapters and all of the chapters contained in the first edition have been completely revised. New material has been incorporated and various clarifications regarding diverse points critical to mission have been made. However, the intention remains the same as when the first edition was published in 1997. There we expressed that this book was written "with the sole purpose of dialoging publicly with all those who are committed to the mission of God in distinct social, political, and cultural frontiers." The intention has not changed. It is my prayer that the Lord of mission will help us in this urgent task of publicly proclaiming to all human audiences our unbreakable faith in the crucified and risen Jesus of Nazareth.

Darío López Rodríguez
Villa María del Triunfo, October 2003

1

The Liberating Mission of Jesus

The publication of Hans Conzelmann's book *Die Mitte der Zeit: Studien zur Theologie des Lukas* (*The Theology of St. Luke*) in 1953 generated a great deal of debate in academic circles dealing with New Testament exegesis.[1] In more recent years, other authors have paid particular attention to Lucan theology and literature focused on the writings of Luke has notably increased. It can be affirmed that the two books written by Luke, the third gospel and the book of Acts, are now in the crossfire of academic debate[2] and are the focus of study for contemporary specialists

---

1. Conzelmann holds that: "It is not until Luke that this demarcation, this distinction between then and now, the period of Jesus and the period of the Church, between the problems of yesterday and those of today, becomes fully conscious. The period of Jesus and the period of the Church are presented as different epochs in the broad course of saving history, differentiated to some extent by their particular characteristics. . . . The period of Jesus and the period of the Church are represented as two distinct, but systematically interrelated epochs. . . . Luke is confronted by the situation in which the Church finds herself by the delay of the Parousia and her existence in secular history, and he tries to come to terms with the situation by his account of historical events" (*Theology of St. Luke*, 13–14).

2. Marshall, *Luke*, 13.

of sacred Scripture.[3] What are the key themes that Lucan theology articulates? What pastoral challenges and what guidelines for mission emerge from these key themes?

One of the important theological themes that special attention has been dedicated to in the field of biblical studies is the Lucan concept of salvation.[4] Luke uses this word in reference to the content of the good news of the kingdom of God proclaimed by Jesus the carpenter from Nazareth, good news that implies liberation from all oppression. From the Lucan perspective, salvation is an experience accessible to all human beings, and he thus highlights the theme of the universality of mission. But Luke also points out that God has a special love for the poor and the marginalized, including the fragile, those on the periphery, the needy and the destitute, the ragged of the world, and the "nobodies" that predominant society has condemned to social ostracism and the basement of history.

With this debate over Luke's work in mind, the proposal highlighted in this study of the message of Luke's gospel is that this gospel presents the liberating mission of Jesus of Nazareth as a paradigm for the individual and collective witness of believers on all social frontiers and in all cultural contexts. It is a proposal based in a specific temporal context in which millions of human beings of all ages are treated as social trash or disposable items by the global North, and as waste and human leftovers that are not worth anything that the invisible hand of the market expels. The central thesis is that a series of theological themes intersect and converge in Luke's gospel, which together articulate an understanding of mission in terms of integral liberation.

---

3. Senior and Stuhlmueller, *Biblical Foundations for Mission*, 255. In the contemporary discussion regarding the mission of the church, Luke's writings occupy an important position. From the point of view of a missiologist: "Another New Testament passage has become very prominent in the debate about a biblical foundation for mission: Luke's rendering of Jesus' sermon in his home synagogue of Nazareth, in which he applied the prophecy of Isaiah 61:1f. to himself and his ministry. . . . This circumstance alone should be sufficient reason for taking a closer look at Luke's understanding of mission" (Bosch, *Transforming Mission*, 84).

4. A topic closely associated with that of salvation is the Lucan concept of conversion. Luke has a particular interest in this topic in his writings. According to a Bible scholar: "The *topics of conversion and forgiveness* are present . . . in Luke's gospel in exceptional proportions . . . ; they reappear in all of the sections of his work, constituting the soul of it all. It is *the message* that the evangelist sends *to his church* and upon which he bases his entire catechism" (Laconi, *San Lucas*, 34, my translation).

THE CURRENT DEBATE REGARDING THE GOSPEL OF LUKE

Even though Luke's gospel has been widely studied from various conceptual frameworks and starting from different hermeneutical foci, the different experts in New Testament studies who belong to distinct confessional Christian families do not always agree on their particular emphases or on the missionary lines of thinking derived from those emphases. The diversity of opinions circulating at the present time seem to have a critical focus on the unique character of the third gospel, particularly on the Lucan understanding of salvation as an inclusive concept that does not leave room for dichotomies between the spiritual and the social or between the individual and the communal.[5]

One of the experts on the Lucan writings, Philip Esler, suggests that Luke develops a theology of poverty influenced by social, political, and economic factors present in his specific historical context.[6] This same author, following the thinking of Peter Berger, points out that this particular work confirms that "the relationship between religion and society is always dialectical."[7] From a missiological perspective, Donald Senior suggests that a key feature of the theology of mission in Luke is the connection between the history of Jesus and the history of the Church; he also highlights the Lucan emphasis on the universality of mission and the continuity with the history of Israel as much as he does the insertion of Jesus in the world of the poor and marginalized.[8] From his point of view:

> Thus for Luke the concept of the Spirit seals the kinship between God's universal will to save, the liberating ministry of Jesus, and the worldwide mission of the church. During the history of Israel that universal potential is hidden in promise: God would one day redeem his people and reverse the oppression suffered by the lowly. . . . During the lifetime of Jesus, God's Spirit begins to fulfill the promise: those in pain are liberated, the poor are cared for, the outcasts and rejected are brought home. . . . By the way he tells the Gospel story, Luke is able to base the scope and character of the church's mission in the person and ministry of Jesus.[9]

---

5. Green, *Gospel of Luke,* 24–25.

6. Esler, *Community and Gospel,* 164–69.

7. Ibid., 2.

8. Senior and Stuhlmueller, *Biblical Foundations for Mission,* 255–69.

9. Ibid., *Biblical Foundations for Mission,* 269.

Donald Senior also points out that the climatic story of the resurrection appearances in Luke 24:44–49 and its echo in Acts 1:3–8 sum up the theological proposition of Luke. Key themes are present in this highly significant text, such as the universal nature of mission, the death and resurrection of Jesus as the peak events in his history, the call to conversion, the promise of forgiveness, and the place of the community of disciples as witnesses empowered by the Holy Spirit.[10]

Howard Marshall, comparing the gospel of Luke with the other synoptic gospels, maintains that in contrast with the gospel of Mark, Luke highlights the nature of the message of Jesus about the kingdom of God as salvation for the lost. He also establishes that while Matthew presents Jesus of Nazareth as the teacher of true justice, Luke focuses more on his action as savior, showing the particular interest that he had in the poor and marginalized.[11] Furthermore, Marshall proposes that: "In his presentation of the ministry of Jesus Luke draws particular attention to the concern of Jesus for outcasts; all the Gospels bear witness to this undoubted historical fact, but it is Luke who takes most delight in drawing attention to it. . . . Another concern of Jesus to which Luke draws attention is his care for the poor and his warnings that the rich who have lived for themselves thereby shut themselves out of the kingdom of God."[12]

For Gustavo Gutiérrez, one of the most challenging aspects of Luke's theological focus is his sensitivity toward the less favored social sectors.[13] Analyzing the condition of exclusion facing women of the culturally Jewish world of the first century, he holds that: "The mere fact that women collaborated with Jesus shows how new and different his attitude toward them was. But this only fed the prejudices and hostility of those who felt threatened by the ministry of a Galilean preacher."[14] This attitude of Jesus of Nazareth toward women, as Gutiérrez himself affirms, represented a real rupture with the dominant social categories of his time.[15]

From another interpretative framework, following the theological proposition of Schottroff and Stegemann, David Bosch suggests that Luke should not really be called the evangelist of the poor. From his point of

---

10. Senior and Stuhlmueller, *Biblical Foundations for Mission*, 269.

11. Marshall, "Luke, Gospel of," 704–5.

12. Ibid., 705.

13. Gutiérrez, *God of Life*, 182.

14. Ibid., 168.

15. Ibid., 168–69.

view, it is more correct to call him the evangelist of the rich, because the desire of Luke is that his readers know that there is hope for the rich as they act and serve in solidarity with the poor and oppressed. According to Bosch, in their conversion to God, the rich and the poor are also converted to one another.[16] Furthermore, he affirms that the Lucan understanding of salvation has six dimensions: economic, social, political, physical, psychological, and spiritual, the first dimension being the one that Luke gives the most attention to in his gospel.[17] He also recognizes that Luke's special interest in the poor and other marginalized groups is a sensitivity portrayed throughout the entire gospel.[18] He maintains that Jesus' mission has three inseparable and indistinguishable emphases: "1. *empowering the weak and lowly*; 2. *healing the sick*; and 3. *saving the lost*."[19] Bosch affirms that "*each of these ministries presupposes the other two*, not only because the lowly, the sick, and the lost were frequently the same people, but also—and more importantly—because it is impossible, even in our own mission today, to be involved in any one of these ministries to the total exclusion of the other two."[20]

Luise Schottroff and Wolfgang Stegemann, when referring to Jesus of Nazareth as the "hope of the poor," specify that the core of his social message in its Lucan version consists of his instructions to the rich and socially privileged.[21] They hold that Luke presents a concrete social objective: "an equal distribution of property within the [Christian] community."[22]

16. Bosch, *Transforming Mission*, 104.

17. Ibid., 117.

18. Ibid., 98.

19. Bosch, "Mission in Jesus' Way," 4. Bosch specifies that in Luke's gospel, the defenseless and the marginalized are the Samaritans, the women, the tax collectors, and the poor (5–7). The poor are primarily the destitute and those below the poverty line. The word poor is also a collective term used to designate those who were at a disadvantage in first century Palestine, such as the captives, the blind, and the lepers (7).

20. Bosch, "Mission in Jesus' Way," 5.

21. Schottroff and Stegemann, *Hope of the Poor*, 116–17. In regards to this, Schottroff and Stegemann affirm that Luke is not an "'evangelist of the poor.' . . . The poor (in the sense of the destitute) are not the focus of his attention, nor is his social program identical with an ethic of undifferentiated almsgiving. He can more correctly be called the 'evangelist of the rich.' This does not mean that he is their pastor who makes the message, 'Jesus, hope of the poor,' attractive to them. It means, rather, that he is an exceptionally keen critic of the rich and wants their conversion, which is possible only by way of radical renunciation (renunciation of half of their possessions) and unpleasant specific actions (risky loans, cancellation of debts, gifts)" (*Hope of the Poor*, 117).

22. Ibid., 117.

William Barclay and F. F. Bruce, aside from recognizing Jesus' ministry among the despised and needy as one of the dominant themes of the third gospel,[23] point out that Luke was the first author of the gospels to situate the history of Jesus and the history of the Christian church within a broader temporal framework. Bruce states that the entire development of the origins of Christianity is placed within the context of contemporary world history.[24] According to Barclay, "Luke is the first man to see the Christian events against the background of world history. . . . For Luke the events of Christianity were not done in a corner; he sees them in the light of history. . . . Luke alone sees the sweep of history, past, present, and future."[25]

David Gooding is of the opinion that Luke presents the history of Jesus in two great moments within which various theological themes are interlaced. In Gooding's proposal, the first moment corresponds to the coming of the Lord from heaven to earth, and the second moment corresponds to his return from earth to heaven. According to Gooding, the transition between the two moments is found in Luke 9:51, a text narrating the beginning of the ascension of Jesus to the city of Jerusalem.[26] Perhaps for this reason, Joseph Fitzmyer emphasizes the geographical perspective present in Luke. This gospel highlights the place of Jerusalem as the city of destination and describes the activity of Jesus as a way or course, as is expressed clearly in the upward movement from Galilee to Jerusalem (Luke 9:51, 19:28) that is notably underlined in this gospel.[27]

This brief discussion of diverse approaches to and interpretive analyses of Luke's gospel shows that various themes intertwine to outline the theological scope of the third gospel, each one of them possessing highly valuable input for the mission of the Church in any political juncture or historical situation. First of all, as the majority of experts acknowledge, one of the dominant theological ideas articulated by the Lucan view of mission is the special love that God has for the poor and marginalized (tax collectors, Samaritans, lepers, women, children, and the sick), in a cultural climate where women were considered as things and children as incomplete human beings. Secondly, the universality of mission is

---

23. Barclay, *Jesus Christ for Today*, 17; Bruce, *Message of the New Testament*, 59.

24. Bruce, *Message of the New Testament*, 51.

25. Barclay, *Jesus Christ for Today*, 15–16.

26. Gooding, *According to Luke*, 9.

27. Fitzmyer, *Gospel According to Luke*, 165, 169.

emphasized. Throughout the gospel, it is pointed out that the good news of the kingdom of God crosses the geographical borders of Palestine as well as religious, cultural, social, political, and economic barriers. Third, it stands out that the gospel author endeavors to connect the events of the history of Jesus and the history of the Church to secular history. According to Luke, God is the Lord of history and of all the nations. In this sense, social processes and political events can be channels through which he manifests his love and justice, reaching all persons, cultures, and nations. In summary, the announcement of the good news of the kingdom of God as hope of integral liberation for the poor and marginalized characterizes much of Luke. Luke underlines, without losing sight of the theme of the universality of mission, the special love that God has for the outcasts, the wretched of society, the disinherited, and those on the periphery of the world.

KEY THEOLOGICAL THEMES

The universality of mission and God's special love for human beings confined to social ostracism, the poor and the marginalized, are two dominant themes of the third gospel. Of course, there are also other themes that form part of the theological proposition of this gospel. One is the theme of the *Holy Spirit*, which is especially present in the infancy narratives (Luke 1–2).[28] The experiences of the virgin Mary (Luke 1:35), the priest Zacharias (Luke 1:67), the elderly Elizabeth, Zacharias' wife (Luke 1:41), the righteous and devout Simeon (Luke 2:25–27), and John the Baptist (Luke 1:15) confirm this observation. Even more, Jesus himself, before beginning his traveling ministry through the cities and villages of marginalized and scorned Galilee (Luke 8:1; cf. Matt 4:23, 9:35; Mark 1:39), had to be anointed with the Holy Spirit (Luke 4:1, 14, 18). And the community of disciples had to be invested with power from on high (Luke 24:49; Acts 2:1–13) before bearing witness to the good news of salvation in Jerusalem, in all of Judea, in Samaria, and to the ends of the earth (Acts 1:8).

28. Carlos Escudero Freire draws this connection in his book *Devolver el Evangelio a los Pobres: A Propósito de Lucas 1–2* (*Returning the Gospel to the Poor: On the Subject of Luke 1–2*). In the books' introduction, he acknowledges that with this title he has "desired to underline the importance that Luke's gospel gives to the marginalized as privileged recipients of Jesus' message, beginning with the first two chapters" (9, my translation).

The *jubilee* is another recurring theme in the third gospel. Luke emphasizes that Jesus came to liberate human beings from all kinds of oppression. The song of Mary is the first indication of this reality (Luke 1:46–55), a reality which is soon proclaimed publicly in the manifesto of Nazareth, which summarizes the Lucan perspective on the liberating mission of Jesus (Luke 4:16–30). On this occasion, Jesus presents his ministry in terms of integral liberation and points out that the action of God is not limited by geographical borders or by cultural or social borders. The examples of the pagan widow of Zarephath (Luke 4:25–26) and of Naaman, a leper of Syrian origin (Luke 4:27), which provoked a violent reaction on the part of the Jews (Luke 4:29), amply illustrate this point of view.

Prayer is another theme present throughout the gospel of Luke.[29] The author of this gospel portrays Jesus in prayer nine times (Luke 3:21; 5:16; 6:12; 9:18, 29; 11:1–4; 22:39–46; 23:34, 46). Two beautiful exclusively Lucan parables also emphasize the centrality of prayer in the life of the disciples (Luke 18:1–8, 9–14). In the words of Barclay: "It is clear that Luke is out to show us the place of prayer in the life of Jesus, and therefore the place of prayer in our own lives. . . . Luke's Gospel is the Gospel of prayer, and is the Gospel for missioners of Jesus, who must also be prayerful."[30]

Other themes articulated in the Lucan theological position include the *traveling ministry* of Jesus of Nazareth through the cities and villages (Luke 4:15, 43–44; 8:1; 13:22), *following* or discipleship as a response to calling (Luke 5:1–11, 27–32; 9:57–62; 14:25–33), the *casting out of demons* as an undeniable dimension of the liberating mission of Jesus (Luke 6:18; 7:21; 8:26–39; 9:37–43; 10:17; 11:14–23; 13:10–17), and the *joy* that accompanies the incomparable experience of encountering the Lord on certain stretches of the road (Luke 1:44, 58; 2:10, 20; 24:41, 52–53).

All of these themes contribute to outlining Luke's theological proposition. However, two key themes are fundamental to capturing the richness of the Lucan theological texture: the universality of mission and God's special love for the poor and marginalized—the needy and defenseless—according to the predominant social and culture categories of the time.[31] Both themes sum up the nature and scope of the liberating mission of Jesus and, when considered together, articulate an indispensible

29. Rigaux, *Historia de Jesús*, 323.

30. Barclay, *Jesus Christ for Today*, 54, 61.

31. Swartley, "Politics or Peace," 20.

theological platform for an integral missionary insertion in the world of the poor and marginalized.

As early as the story of the Messiah's birth, as told uniquely in Luke, these two themes are present. These themes recur throughout the gospel and express Luke's extraordinary concern for human beings outside of the social and religious frame of reference established in first century Palestine. According to Luke, when an angel of the Lord communicates the good news of the birth of the Messiah in Bethlehem to the shepherds, despised folk regarded as habitual thieves, these were the angel's words: "This will be a sign for you: you will find a child wrapped in bands of cloth and lying in a manger" (Luke 2:12). The same idea is found in Luke 2:7 ("And she . . . wrapped him in bands of cloth, and laid him in a manger . . .") and in Luke 2:16 ("So they went with haste and found Mary and Joseph, and the child lying in the manger"). What is the theological significance of this sign, which has two key elements: wrapped in cloths and laid in a manger? The phrase "wrapped in bands of cloth" indicates the identification of the Messiah, from birth, with the entire human being and with all human beings. It constitutes a clear sign of the universality of mission. The phrase "laid in a manger" expresses the identification of the Messiah with all the destitute and defenseless of the world. In having an animal trough as a cradle, a vessel located in an environment of work and sweat, the Messiah entered into solidarity with the outcasts and the excluded, the needy and the destitute, the poor and the marginalized, and those on the periphery.

The Universality of Mission

The universality of mission, or the universality of salvation, is one of the key themes of Lucan theology.[32] The third gospel emphasizes that salvation is extended to all human beings of all cultures, peoples, and nations. This particular aspect of the Lucan theological proposition is notably underlined when, in contrast to the gospel of Matthew, Luke does not begin his genealogy of Jesus of Nazareth with Abraham, the father of the nation of Israel, but rather begins it with Adam (Luke 3:23–38). By this, he insinuates that Jesus came to bring salvation not only to the Jews, but to all of humanity. Key passages such as the parable of the Good Samaritan (Luke 10:25–27), the cleansing of the Samaritan leper (Luke 17:11–19), and the Lucan version of the Great Commission (Luke 24:44–49), support this theological emphasis. Even more, the song of Simeon during

---

32. Rigaux, *Historia de Jesús*, 293–96; Escudero Freire, *Devolver el Evangelio*, 284–85.

the presentation of Jesus in the Jerusalem temple was a clear indicator of this reality (Luke 2:28–32). On that occasion, the just and pious Simeon, who awaited the liberation of Israel (Luke 2:25), publicly declared the following: "Master, now you are dismissing your servant in peace, according to your word; for my eyes have seen your salvation, which you have prepared in the presence of all peoples, a light for revelation to the Gentiles and for glory to your people Israel" (Luke 2:29–32).

This key text shows that Simeon understood the advent of the Messiah as the fulfillment of the promise that all of the peoples would be witnesses to the powerful intervention of the Lord in history to liberate his people. But that was not all, as he himself testifies that his eyes have seen the *Christós kúrios* or the Anointed of the Lord (Luke 2:26), the Messiah that would be "a light for revelation to the Gentiles" (Luke 2:32) or "a light to the nations" (Isa 42:6). The close relation of the song of Simeon to Isa 42:1–9 cannot be denied. In light of the greater theological context in which this song is situated, this prophetic declaration signifies the affirmation that the coming of the Messiah would bring "justice to the nations" (Isa 42:1).

When Jesus publicly proclaimed the distinguishing characteristics of his liberating mission, in the passage known as the Messianic platform or the manifesto of Nazareth (Luke 4:16–30), the mention of two non-Jews—the pagan widow of Zarephath and Naaman the Syrian who suffered from leprosy—whose stories are recorded in the Old Testament (1 Kgs 17:8–24; 2 Kgs 5:1–19), undoubtedly indicated that the Gentiles were included in God's plan of salvation. Luke, in his account of the events, emphasizes that the Jews present at the synagogue in Nazareth clearly understood the meaning of Jesus' words and for that reason: "When they heard this, all in the synagogue were filled with rage. They got up, drove him out of the town, and led him to the brow of the hill on which their town was built, so that they might hurl him off the cliff" (Luke 4:28–29).

As this biblical text indicates, due to the provincial mentality and the cultural and religious ethnocentrism of his audience, it turned out to be extremely offensive and shocking that the son of Joseph (Luke 4:22) publicly declared that two non-Jews, a pagan woman from Zarephath and a leper of Syrian origin, were human beings worthy of God's love. But the intention of Luke's account was more than that. The idea behind the reference to these two foreigners is that from the time of the Old Testament, it was already clear that God was not the exclusive property of any one culture, people, or race. Thus, during the exposition of his Messianic program rooted in the principles of the jubilee, Jesus affirmed that all human beings—Jews and non-Jews—were recipients of the good news of liberation. And it should not be forgotten that the speech at the synagogue in Nazareth is a condensed version of the gospel[33] and acts as a key that captures the theological proposition underlined in Luke's account of the history of Jesus, just as Acts 1:8 does for the history of the missionary advance of the church.

Luke's version of the healing of the centurion's servant in effect confirms that the good news of the kingdom of God was also within reach of those who were not Jews (Luke 7:1–10). The story is very thought-provoking, principally due to the final words of Jesus after having listened to the reasons that the representative of the Roman Empire gave in order to have his concrete need taken care of:

> When he heard about Jesus, he sent some Jewish elders to him, asking him to come and heal his slave. When they came to Jesus, they appealed to him earnestly, saying, "He is worthy of having you do this for him, for he loves our people, and it is he who built our synagogue for us." And Jesus went with them, but when he was not far from the house, the centurion sent friends to say to him, "Lord, do not trouble yourself, for I am not worthy to have you come under my roof; therefore I did not presume to come to you. But only speak the word, and let my servant be healed. For I also am a man set under authority, with soldiers under me; and I say to one, 'Go,' and he goes, and to another, 'Come,' and he comes, and to my slave, 'Do this,' and the slave does it." When Jesus heard this he was amazed at him, and turning to the crowd that followed him, he said, "I tell you, not even in Israel have I found such faith" (Luke 7:3–9).

This account emphasizes two important pieces of information. First of all, it draws attention to the fact that some Jewish leaders ("elders") considered this foreign soldier worthy of having his petition granted by the Lord (Luke 7:4). Their reasons were clear enough: "For he loves our people, and it is he who built our synagogue for us" (Luke 7:5). Secondly, it calls attention to the fact that the faith and humble attitude of this foreign soldier were publicly recognized by Jesus: "'Not even in Israel have I found such faith'" (Luke 7:9). Was this a subtle critique of the lack of spiritual

33. Bosch, *Transforming Mission*, 89.

sensitivity of some Jews to recognize the presence of the Messiah in the midst of their people? The continuing controversies that Jesus had with the Jewish leaders regarding various subjects relating to the purpose of the day of rest (Luke 6:6–11; 13:10–17) appear to confirm that, in accounts like the healing of the centurion's servant, there was in effect a subtle critique of the lack of faith of the scribes and Pharisees.

Luke also presents the example of the queen of the South who came to listen to the wisdom of Solomon and the example of the inhabitants of Nineveh who repented of their sins following Jonah's preaching (Luke 11:29–32) as signs of judgment for a perverse generation that did not recognize what was *for its peace* (Luke 19:42) nor the *time of its visitation* (Luke 19:44), two references closely associated with the presence and task of the Messiah on the stage of history. In Luke's gospel, Gentile individuals and peoples are given as examples of openness to God's voice, contrasting their faith with the hardness of heart of the scribes and Pharisees.

Another text with important missionary content is the account of the healing of the ten lepers (Luke 17:11–19). It is incredibly significant that such emphasis is placed on the gratitude of the Samaritan, a despicable foreigner to the Jews, in contrast with the ungrateful attitude of the other nine lepers, who were probably all of Jewish nationality. Luke underlines that only the Samaritan glorified "God with a loud voice. He prostrated himself at Jesus' feet" (Luke 17:15–16). Two things in this text are noteworthy. The first is that the ministry of Jesus has also reached the Samaritans, a mixed race, hated and scorned by the Jews. The second notable fact is that this Samaritan, whom Jesus recognized as a foreigner, responded with gratitude to the miracle of the Lord in his life. In other words, unlike the other nine lepers who were also cured by Jesus, only a Samaritan foreigner was sensitive to the love of God. The questions formulated by Jesus and his final words are aptly eloquent, showing the way in which he valued and treated this grateful foreigner: "Then Jesus asked, 'Were not ten made clean? But the other nine, where are they? Was none of them found to return and give praise to God except this foreigner?' Then he said to him, "Get up and go on your way; your faith has made you well" (Luke 17:17–19).

According to the Lucan account, the Samaritan was liberated not only from the disease of leprosy which Jewish law considered as impure, but also from his condition of social ostracism. In light of the Lucan concept of salvation, when this man, doubly excluded due to being a

Samaritan and suffering from leprosy, had an encounter with Jesus in a village located between Samaria and Galilee, he was integrally liberated. In addition to freeing him from the terrible disease of leprosy, the salvation granted by Jesus also reinserted him into society.

The parable of the Good Samaritan (Luke 10:25–37) marks another key moment outlining the Lucan perspective on the universality of mission. Faced with the important theological questions of an interpreter of the law ("Teacher . . . what must I do to inherit eternal life? . . . And who is my neighbor?"), Jesus responded by comparing the reactions of a Levite and of a priest who were descending from Jerusalem, both representatives of the Jewish people, with the reaction of a Samaritan to the compelling situation of a man along the road who was "half dead." According to the story, while the first two passed by "on the other side," only the Samaritan was "moved with pity." In this Lucan parable, the generosity of the Samaritan expressed itself in concrete actions of love, from bandaging the wounds and carrying the wounded, to caring for him and spending his time and money seeking the well-being of his neighbor. The generosity of the Samaritan in the parable explains why Jesus used him as an example of mercy and as a model of a neighbor. In this context, the words of Jesus to the interpreter of the law ("Go and do likewise") were a public critique of the narrow mentality and the prejudices of the religious elite, who limited the love of God to the borders of Palestine and the concept of neighbor to their co-nationals. A reading of this parable that takes into account the Lucan perspective of salvation reveals that it emphasizes the inclusivity of God's love, as a scorned and hated Samaritan, who according to the then current opinion of many Jews was neither a neighbor nor capable of acting as a neighbor, against every expectation acted as a neighbor.

The declaration of the resurrected Christ (Luke 24:44–49), which is based in the prophecies of the Old Testament relating to the person and the work of the Messiah, clearly establishes the universal character of mission. Luke records with these words his unique version of the Great Commission: "Then he opened their minds to understand the scriptures, and he said to them, 'Thus it is written, that the Messiah is to suffer and to rise from the dead on the third day, and that repentance and the forgiveness of sins is to be proclaimed in his name to all the nations, beginning from Jerusalem'" (Luke 24:45–47).

This profoundly significant text confirms that God's mission has a universal reach. God's mission transcends the geographic borders of Israel, thereby questioning cultural prejudices imposed by some Jewish traditions. In this sense, the horizon of the message of repentance and forgiveness of sins in the name of Jesus was and continues to be all of the nations (*pánta tá éthnos*, Luke 24:47). The book of Acts amply corroborates this perspective, as it testifies to the missionary expansion of the church in the first century, beginning from Jerusalem and reaching to the capitol of the Roman Empire.

The missionary route outlined by Luke in his gospel indicates that there is no such thing as a prohibited place or space, whether social or physical, for the evangelizing action and social engagement of the church. This is the case because if salvation is inclusive in character, the natural correlate to this affirmation is that the missional vocation of the church surpasses any limiting theological or ideological factor. According to Luke, all of the cultural, religious, social, political, and economic frontiers are natural spaces of mission for the people of God. In all of these places and structures of society, the gospel of the kingdom of God must be announced daily by witnesses empowered by the Holy Spirit. The will of God is that all persons and all peoples know his purpose of salvation. God is light for all of the nations. The message of repentance and the forgiveness of sins must be proclaimed and lived in every place where a human being in need of the grace of God is found. In this sense, it is profoundly significant that the Lucan narrative of the crucifixion and death of Jesus underlines that, in this dramatic moment, one of the evildoers or thieves (a marginalized person), received a promise from Jesus: "Truly I tell you, today you will be with me in Paradise" (Luke 23:43). There it is also recorded that at the foot of the cross, a Roman centurion (a foreigner) recognized that Jesus was righteous: "When the centurion saw what had taken place, he praised God and said, 'Certainly this man was innocent'" (Luke 23:47).[34] In other words, at this decisive hour, at the foot of the cross, two human beings representative of two distinct and distant social sectors, a marginalized person like the thief and an official of the Roman Empire like the centurion, were confronted with the liberating message of Jesus. In light of all of these facts, it is sufficiently clear that the disciples of Jesus of Nazareth are permanently challenged to be like

---

34. The other synoptic gospels indicate that the Roman centurion recognized that Jesus was the Son of God (Matt 27:54; Mark 15:39).

the Good Samaritan of the parable, as passing by on the other side when faced with the spiritual and social needs of human beings of flesh and bone, as the priest and the Levite did, signifies a negation of the liberating nature of the gospel and a betrayal of the integral missional vocation of the church. Consequently, being like Jesus, who extended his love to the Samaritans, despised and segregated by the pious Jews, means weaving a path of hope and joy in a temporal setting marked by forms of subtle and open violence that spurn the dignity and the rights of the fragile and needy of society. According to Lucan testimony, the God of life demands his disciples to put aside their theological, political, and cultural prejudices that objectify human beings.

God's Special Love for the Poor and the Marginalized

The special love that God has for the exiles of the earth—the needy and the defenseless, the weak and the oppressed,[35] those on the periphery and the disinherited, the scorned who are treated as disposable trash or social waste—is one of the dominant theological themes of Luke's gospel. From the beginning of the story of Jesus, Luke highlights the particular concern that God has for the social sectors considered as leftover or disposable according to some religious regulations and cultural standards of the first century. God includes the excluded.[36] In the infancy narrative this emphasis, characteristic of the third gospel, can already be perceived.[37] Indeed, both the *Magnificat* (Luke 1:46–55) and the *Benedictus* (Luke 1:67–79) emphasize the powerful intervention of God in history to enact justice for the weak and to bring salvation to the just and devout (Luke 1:6; 2:25) who were awaiting the consolation of Israel (Luke 2:25) and the redemption of Jerusalem (Luke 2:38). In other words, from the beginning of his gospel, Luke indicates that the social sectors placed on the other bank of history, those humble before God like Zechariah, Elizabeth, Mary, Simeon, and Anna, were the most receptive to the voice of the Lord. Poor and unsophisticated folk, such as the scorned shepherds, were the first recipients of the good news of the advent of the Messiah (Luke 2:8–11). Moreover, here it is underlined that two defenseless children, considered as insignificant and as incomplete human beings according

---

35. O'Toole, "Luke's Position on Politics," 4, 9.

36. Craddock, *Luke*, 78.

37. Escudero Freire, *Devolver el Evangelio*, 9.

to the predominant cultural standards of the first century, came to fulfill the Old Testament prophecies regarding the liberating mission of the Messiah (Luke 1:68–80; 2:10–11, 27–32).

In his gospel Luke specifies that Jesus began his ministry traveling through cities and villages preaching the gospel of the kingdom of God in the underdeveloped province of Galilee (Luke 4:14, 15, 42–43; 8:1). It was in the synagogue of Nazareth, a village located in the marginal and spurned Galilee, where he expounded his messianic program (Luke 4:16–30), in which he specified that he had come "to proclaim the year of the Lord's favor" (Luke 4:19) or the jubilee. On that occasion, before an exclusively Jewish audience, he proclaimed a message of integral liberation with clear social and political consequences.

According to Yoder: "Here the passage from Isaiah 61 which Jesus turns upon himself is not only a most explicitly messianic one: it is one which states the messianic expectation in the most expressly social terms."[38] From Yoder's perspective, it is highly probable that these messianic expectations were associated with the egalitarian impact of the Sabbath year or jubilee.[39] In other words, the Jesus' pronouncement in the synagogue of Nazareth had a very explicit social and political content. The Messiah had come to proclaim good news to the poor: *euangelizō ptōchos* (Luke 4:18). It is worth noting that this declaration began in the underdeveloped province of Galilee, a region populated by a mixed race that the pious of Jerusalem despised, an area inhabited by hundreds of widows, orphans, poor, and unemployed.[40] From Galilee began the announcement of the good news of liberation to the poor and oppressed (Luke 4:18).

In regards to this, Jesus' reply to the disciples of John the Baptist is incredibly eloquent: "When the men had come to him, they said, 'John the Baptist has sent us to you to ask, "Are you the one who is to come, or are we to wait for another?"' Jesus had just then cured many people of diseases, plagues, and evil spirits, and had given sight to many who were blind. And he answered them, 'Go and tell John what you have seen and heard: the blind receive their sight, the lame walk, the lepers are cleansed, the deaf hear, the dead are raised, and the poor [*ptōchos*] have good news brought to them'" (Luke 7:20–22).

---

38. Yoder, *Politics of Jesus*, 34–35.

39. Ibid., 36.

40. Saracco, "Liberating Options of Jesus," 33–41; Gutiérrez, *God of Life*, 99–100.

Scorned Galilee was the geographic location where the liberating mission of Jesus began. And it was precisely in a synagogue in marginal Galilee where Jesus expounded his messianic program.[41] But beyond these facts that are significant to capturing the theological texture of the liberating mission of Jesus, in contrast to the other gospels, the distinguishing characteristic of Luke's gospel is that it highlights Jesus' permanent relationship and contact with the poor and the oppressed. In the words of Gustavo Gutiérrez: "Luke is the evangelist who is most sensitive to social realities. In his Gospel as well as in Acts the themes of material poverty, of goods held in common, and of the condemnation of the rich are frequently treated."[42]

In the same sense, Howard Marshall holds that Luke's gospel emphasizes the special concern that Jesus has for those who are underprivileged: the poor, women, children, and those declared sinners.[43] Undoubtedly, one of the central theological themes of Luke is the presentation of the ministry of Jesus as the proclamation of the good news of liberation to the poor and the marginalized. The cumulative evidence present in this gospel is sufficiently solid. Yoder has performed an original exegesis of passages on this subject (Luke 1:46ff., 68ff.; 3:21—4:14; 4:14ff.; 6:12ff.; 9:1–22; 12:49—13:9; 14:25–36; 19:36–46; 22:24–53), aptly demonstrating the social and political implications of the Lucan theological focus.[44]

---

41 The gospels of Matthew and Mark also testify to Jesus' Galilean Option. The proclamation of the good news of the kingdom of God began in Galilee (Matt 4:12–23; Mark 1:14–15), the first disciples were called along the shores of the Lake of Galilee (Matt 4:18–25; Mark 1:16–20), and it was in Galilee that Jesus appeared to his disciples (Mark 16:6–7) and gave them the task of proclaiming the gospel to all the nations (Matt 28:16–20). All of these facts undoubtedly stand in contrast to the general opinion that Jews had regarding Galilee: "Can anything good come out of Nazareth?" (John 1:46); "Surely you are not also from Galilee, are you? Search and you will see that no prophet is to arise from Galilee" (John 7:52). Within this same interpretive framework—Jesus' Galilean Option—two events are noteworthy. First, in the revelation of Saul of Tarsus on the road to Damascus, the Lord presented himself as Jesus of Nazareth: "I am Jesus of Nazareth whom you are persecuting" (Acts 22:8). Second, in their preaching and testimony, the community of disciples publicly identified with the Galilean preacher who had been crucified: "Let it be known to all of you, and to all the people of Israel, that this man is standing before you in good health by the name of Jesus Christ of Nazareth, whom you crucified, whom God raised from the dead" (Acts 4:10).

42. Gutiérrez, *Theology of Liberation*, 170.

43. Marshall, *Luke*, 138–41.

44. Yoder, *Politics of Jesus*, 26–63.

Yoder also suggests that passages like the *Magnificat* present "the maiden Myriam as a Maccabean."[45]

But who are the poor and the marginalized in Luke's gospel? Accurately establishing the basic characteristics that defined the poor and the marginalized sectors and the limits of the social space in which they could mobilize does not prove to be an easy task. In spite of these difficulties certain theological, cultural, and political factors are of immense usefulness in explaining which of the social sectors we are referring to when we speak of the poor and the marginalized. In first century Palestine the world of the marginalized was composed primarily of lepers, tax collectors or publicans, Samaritans, women, the sick, and children. Each of these social sectors was condemned to social ostracism. In other words, in a society marked by the insensitive religious values of Pharisees and the petty political interests of scribes and Sadducees, the levels of marginalization were economic (the poor), social (women, children, the sick, and tax collectors), cultural (Samaritans, women, and children), and religious (women, tax collectors, Samaritans, and the sick). Within this context, although the poor formed part of the world of the marginalized, not all of the marginalized formed part of the world of the poor.

Thus the publicans Zacchaeus and Matthew were not poor in the material sense of the term, but they occupied a space in the world of the marginalized and the excluded of their time. Due to their condition as tax collectors linked to the imperial power, both Matthew and Zacchaeus were marginalized in Jewish society. As this was the case, it is possible to understand why the scribes and Pharisees murmured when Jesus and his disciples entered into the homes of publicly recognized sinners like Matthew and Zacchaeus. The case of Levi or Matthew illustrates this point: "Then Levi gave a great banquet for him in his house; and there was a large crowd of tax collectors and others sitting at the table with them. The Pharisees and their scribes were complaining to his disciples, saying, 'Why do you eat and drink with tax collectors and sinners?" (Luke 5:29–30). Regarding Jesus' presence in the house of the tax collector Zacchaeus, it is similarly underlined that: "All who saw it began to grumble and said, 'He has gone to be the guest of one who is a sinner'" (Luke 19:7).

Likewise many of the women, culturally and religiously marginalized as such, who followed Jesus had material possessions that placed them as members of a socially privileged sector. Joanna, the wife of Herod's

45. Ibid., 26.

steward Cuza, and Susanna, among other women who served Jesus with their resources (Luke 8:3), are examples that illustrate this affirmation. Although we do not have detailed information regarding the social and economic condition of each of the lepers, the sick, the possessed, the Samaritans, and the other non-Jews with whom Jesus had contact, it is probable that the majority of them socially, culturally, and economically formed part of the world of the material poor. Taking into account the previously mentioned examples of the tax collectors and women, it can be maintained that not all of the marginalized with whom Jesus dealt and related were poor in the material sense of the term, as in the case of the publicans Zacchaeus and Matthew and the women Joanna and Susanna.[46]

Consequently, when we speak of the marginalized, first we refer to the poor in the sociological and economic sense of the term—that is, to the immense contingent of human beings that inhabit social spaces marked by subhuman living conditions, with defined material needs and with political and economic prospects that are limited by the selfishness of the dominant sectors. We speak basically of the material poor that live beneath the poverty line and do not have what is necessary for daily subsistence.[47] Second, we refer to the sectors or subcultures that are considered marginal within any social or political system. This was the case of the tax collectors and lepers in the cultural world of Palestine during Jesus' ministry. Nevertheless, in defiance of the social and cultural categories of his time, Jesus tied himself permanently with the needy and the scorned of society.

46. The same occurs today. Those with AIDS, homosexuals, drug addicts, prostitutes, the disabled, and delinquents, among other marginalized groups, are present in all social sectors. In this sense, marginality is currently also a complex problem that crosses all types of boundaries.

47. The Greek word *ptōchos*, which appears thirty-four times in all of the New Testament, refers chiefly to the destitute, needy of what is essential to live (Gutiérrez, *Theology of Liberation*, 170). This term is used ten times in Luke's gospel to designate those persons who live in a social situation characterized by a deficiency or absence of material goods (4:19; 6:20; 7:22; 14:13, 21; 16:20, 22; 18:22; 19:8; 21:3). In contrast to the gospels of Mark and Matthew, in which the term *ptōchos* appears five times, in Luke it occurs ten times. Bosch affirms that in Luke poverty is primarily a social category and *ptōchos* is usually a collective term for all who find themselves in a situation of disadvantage (*Transforming Mission*, 99). Beda Rigaux affirms that: "The poor person magnified by Luke is not the one who is poor *in spirit*. It is the one who is truly in need and is spurned because of his or her material condition. . . . The poor are those who hunger now (Luke 6:20–21, 24–25)" (*Historia de Jesús*, 299, my translation).

This explains why the scribes and Pharisees criticized Jesus at different moments, accusing him of being a friend of publicans and sinners (Luke 7:34; 15:1–2). Jesus' association with individuals who were undervalued and excluded by society also explains the reasons why the representatives of Jewish society saw the ministry of the Galilean preacher as a permanent threat to their religious interests and their particular political interests. Moreover, the reiterated references to the systemic opposition and the conspiracy of the scribes and Pharisees (Luke 6:7–11; 7:49; 11:53–54; 14:1–6; 19:47–48; 20:1–8, 19–40; 22:1–6; 23:1–25) account for the discomfort of the leaders when faced with the proclamation of the kingdom of God by Jesus, which Luke insistently points out throughout his gospel (Luke 4:43; 6:20; 7:28; 8:1, 10; 9:2, 11, 27, 60, 62; 10:9, 11; 11:2, 20; 12:31–32; 13:18–20, 28–29; 14:15; 16:16; 17:20–21; 18:16–17, 24–25; 29; 21:31; 22:16–18, 29–30). But beyond this atmosphere of continual tension, Luke presents us with a Jesus who sits at the table with the hated publicans and invites one of them to be his disciple, who has contact with the lepers considered as unclean, and who has various women among his followers. As Donald Senior has observed:

> Although Jesus the prophet does minister within Israel, the style of his ministry retains the limitless potential announced at Nazareth. He befriends and shares table fellowship with tax collectors and sinners. . . . More than any other evangelist Luke emphasizes Jesus' association with women—a stunning crossing of a social and religious barrier in the patriarchal society of his day. The Lucan Jesus is open to "official" outsiders such as the Gentile centurion . . . and Samaritans. . . . Jesus reaches out to lepers . . . and care for the poor is a constant theme of his preaching.[48]

Luke also insistently highlights the liberating mission of Jesus on the day of rest (Luke 4:31–37; 6:6–11; 13:10–17; 14:1–6). This was one of the factors that provoked the angry reaction of the scribes and Pharisees. From that moment, they began to seek motives to kill Jesus. The passage on the healing of the man with a withered hand, a disabled person, is highly paradigmatic.

> On another sabbath he entered the synagogue and taught, and there was a man whose right hand was withered. The scribes and the Pharisees watched him to see whether he would cure on the

---

48. Senior and Stuhlmueller, *Biblical Foundations for Mission*, 261.

sabbath, so that they might find an accusation against him. . . .
But they were filled with fury and discussed with one another
what they might do to Jesus (Luke 6:6–7, 11).

The biblical texts that record the controversies regarding the day
of rest contrast the difference between Jesus' understanding of the significance of this day with the theological short-sightedness of the scribes
and the Pharisees that limited the love of God to six days of the week.
The words of the leader of the synagogue where Jesus healed the woman
who had been crippled for eighteen years amply illustrate the theological
perspective of the scribes and the Pharisees regarding this issue: "There
are six days on which work ought to be done; come on those days and
be cured, and not on the sabbath day" (Luke 13:14). In contrast to this
representative of the established religion, for Jesus the sabbath was a day
of affirmation of life and of valorization of human dignity: "I ask you,
is it lawful to do good or to do harm on the sabbath, to save life or to
destroy it?" (Luke 6:9). From Jesus' perspective, the day of rest was also
a legitimate time to unfasten the bonds of oppression: "And ought not
this woman, a daughter of Abraham whom Satan bound for eighteen
long years, be set free from this bondage on the sabbath day?" (Luke
13:16). The relevance of this passage rests on the questions formulated
by Jesus—words that denounced both the values of a society that had
placed its religious prejudices and cultural practices above the value of
human life and the lack of mercy from the religious folk who considered
themselves to be pious.

Various stories recorded by Luke in his gospel can be analyzed with
the intention of ironing out the central theological ideas and ethical challenges that are presented as constant themes in Jesus' relation to the poor
and marginalized of his time. The account of the calling of Matthew is
one of them (Luke 5:27–32). In this passage the connection between *going* and *seeing* is particularly noteworthy. When Jesus went to walk by the
sea he saw Matthew immersed in his daily work, which means that Jesus
did not encounter Matthew outside of his regular work environment.
The invitation to follow him occurred within the bounds of his marginal
space: "sitting at the tax booth" (Luke 5:27). A concrete lesson can be derived from this. In order to see and to know, to discover the world of the
marginalized, we have to come out of our narrow theological and limited
and limiting cultural settings. We have to cross borders and barriers that
impede us from submerging ourselves in the world of those excluded by

the prevailing system and we have to insert ourselves visibly into critical social spaces. Words are not sufficient.

The acceptance of the invitation to eat at the same table with publicans and sinners, under the roof of someone excluded by the system (Matthew or Levi), marks another key missionary principle. In this sense, solidarity with the marginalized must be more than an interesting theological discourse or outstanding ideological proposal. It must be a daily experience that runs the risk of publicly identifying with the socially and culturally marginalized sectors. Consequently, sitting and the same table and breaking the bread in communion with the disinherited of this world forms part of a missionary approach that has, as its point of departure, an encounter with one's neighbor on some stretch of the road.

Accordingly, there are five principles that mold the chain of self-giving love: going, seeing, compassion, commitment, and transformation.[49] These five principles are more than simple steps in a hermeneutic process or a formula for walking among the poor and marginalized; they constitute and mark out a way of life that recognizes the other not as an object or thing, but as a subject with dignity and rights. Regarding this, the words of Jesus in response to the slander of the scribes and Pharisees are quite explicit:

> The Pharisees and their scribes were complaining to his disciples, saying, "Why do you eat and drink with tax collectors and sinners?" Jesus answered, "Those who are well have no need of a physician, but those who are sick; I have come to call not the righteous but sinners to repentance" (Luke 5:30–32).

The biblical text that narrates the offering of the poor widow (Luke 21:1–4) also outlines valuable missional principles. Once again, the action of *seeing* as a way of *knowing* what occurs in a social environment is essential to understanding the pedagogy of Jesus. It is a *seeing* that knows how to differentiate between the religious motivations and practices of the rich and of a very poor widow. Luke emphasizes that this is a way of seeing that transcends the world of appearances and discerns and values the intentions of the heart more than the power of money. The triply marginalized widow—because she was a woman, a widow, and very poor

---

49. René Padilla, when referring to what he calls the chain of self-giving love, specifies that this chain has three principles: seeing, having compassion, and acting ("Ser Prójimo," 148). Guillermo Cook prefers to use the trinomial: seeing, judging, and acting ("Ver, Juzgar y Actuar," 96).

(*penicrós*)—trusted in God as the God of life. The offering of the two copper coins of insignificant monetary value in the exchange market and the business world expressed the richness of a humble faith that hoped in God. The widow did not give out of what she had in surplus but out of what she needed to survive that day. In other words, she gave all that she had for her sustenance, trusting solely in the mercy of the God of life. With this beautiful example of commitment as far as the utmost consequences, Jesus challenges us to be like this very poor widow and not like the many rich that live based on appearances, converting this type of faith into a cheap commodity. An extremely poor woman, triply marginalized, was given as a paradigm for gospel spirituality, underlining that God was a daily reality for her. The example of this very poor widow clearly establishes that trusting in God as the God of life frees us from the love of money: "He said, 'Truly I tell you, this poor widow has put in more than all of them; for all of them have contributed out of their abundance, but she out of her poverty has put in all she had to live on'" (Luke 21:3–4).

The condition of poverty and the situation of marginality are not, or should not be, impediments to doing theology. The experience of this poor widow indicates that a theological proposition that proclaims and confesses God as the God of life can be articulated from the periphery of society. The cases of Matthew and of the poor widow are two paradigms for the missionary commitment of the church today. Both accounts, which are found also in the gospels of Matthew (9:9–13) and Mark (2:13–17), are connected to the Lucan emphasis on the special love that God has for the outlying social sectors. They have implications and theological significance essential to the mission of the church at the present historical juncture.

In addition, Lucan texts like the parables of the wedding guests (Luke 14:7–14), the great banquet (Luke 14:15–24), and the rich man and Lazarus (Luke 16:19–31) penetrate the theological significance of God's special love for the excluded and dispossessed. The parables of the lost sheep (Luke 15:1–7) and the prodigal son (Luke 15:11–32) also clearly testify to this special love for the disinherited. From another angle, the paradigmatic and singular cases of the rich young ruler (Luke 18:18–30) and of Zacchaeus, a chief tax collector (Luke 19:1–10), give an account of two ways in which the rich respond to the invitation of Jesus. According to Luke, the rich do not remain off to the side, but the accent of this gospel falls on the others, the forgotten who are picked up along the road, as is expressed in the parable of the great banquet:

> "The owner of the house . . . said to his slave, 'Go out at once into the streets and lanes of the town and bring in the poor, the crippled, the blind, and the lame.' And the slave said, 'Sir, what you ordered has been done, and there is still room.' Then the master said to the slave, 'Go out into the roads and the lanes, and compel people to come in, so that my house may be filled. For I tell you, none of those who were invited will taste my dinner'" (Luke 14:21–24).

Thus it remains clear that in Luke's gospel the poor and the marginalized are human beings worthy of the love of God and are missional subjects. The special love that God has for these excluded and scorned social sectors constitutes a constant missional challenge for the disciples of the crucified and risen Lord who are within a religious camp saturated with theological propositions that see objects and things rather than human beings with dignity and rights. Seeing and acting like the Good Samaritan is the concrete missional model that Luke proposes. Moreover, from the Lucan perspective, sitting at the table of marginal folk like publicans and surrendering two small coins as an offering according to the example of the poor widow are more than mere missional methods or alternative ways of serving one's neighbor—they constitute concrete forms of assuming a Galilean Option that confesses and celebrates God as the God of life.

Following the way of Jesus, submerging oneself in the world of the forgotten, knowing their hopes and despairs from within, being in solidarity with them in the fight for a democratization of politics and economy, and identifying with their daily needs may cause others to accuse us and say of us: "Look, a glutton and a drunkard, a friend of tax collectors and sinners!" (Luke 7:34). This may be the cost of following Jesus within a conservative ecclesiastical climate that does not look highly upon the defense of the human rights of the disinherited and a firm commitment to social justice. Prophetically denouncing provincialism, hypocrisy, and the lack of mercy of contemporary Pharisees may provoke political reactions that put at risk the personal security of believers who value proclaiming the fullness of the gospel over complying with popular theological discourse and selling out to the dominant ideology of the contemporary religious market. Luke is sufficiently clear in regards to this

when he narrates the reaction of the scribes and the Pharisees to Jesus'
public denouncement of their religious hypocrisy:

> "But woe to you Pharisees! For you tithe mint and rue and herbs
> of all kinds, and neglect justice and the love of God; it is these
> you ought to have practiced, without neglecting the others. Woe
> to you Pharisees! For you love to have the seat of honor in the
> synagogues and to be greeted with respect in the marketplaces.
> Woe to you! For you are like unmarked graves, and people walk
> over them without realizing it." . . .
>   When he went outside, the scribes and the Pharisees began
> to be very hostile toward him and to cross-examine him about
> many things, lying in wait for him, to catch him in something he
> might say (Luke 11:42–44, 53–54).

In sum, the cost of discipleship should never lead us to lower the
demands of the gospel, to fear proclaiming the good news of liberation to
all human audiences and at all historical junctures, to change the purpose
of God that every knee should bow and tongue confess Jesus as Lord,
to limit the concrete implications of the universal nature of the mission
that crosses all social and cultural frontiers, or to be ignorant of God's
special love for the poor and the marginalized due to our own theological
prejudices.

CONCLUSIONS

The liberating mission of Jesus has a universal reach. The proclamation
of the gospel of the kingdom of God crosses frontiers of every kind. The
poor and the marginalized are both subjects and agents of God's mission. This means that within the world of poverty and marginality, we
must set up a permanent missional tent as a space for solidarity and
as an open channel for the collective search for justice. The good news
of liberation, a message for all human beings and for all peoples, has a
double effect. First, it transforms and integrally liberates all human beings who respond to the call of Jesus and obey the demands of the gospel,
joyfully taking on the cost of discipleship. Second, it relativizes social,
political, and economic structures that objectify human beings created
in the image of God, and it exposes dehumanizing religious and cultural
prejudices. The Lucan perspective of Jesus' mission proposes a platform
of action that is profoundly relevant for the insertion of the church into

all missional frontiers. God's special love for the poor and the marginalized is one of the key theological themes that Luke outlines and proposes as an inescapable agenda item for the church's mission. In this sense, even though we interpret the missional demands of Luke's gospel in different ways according to our theological and political perspectives, we cannot ignore that one of the central emphases of this gospel is the affirmation of God's special love for the poor and the marginalized. Luke stresses that believers must be like the Good Samaritan and like the poor widow. The disciples of Jesus of Nazareth are not called to be indifferent or to pass by on the other side when faced with real needs of human beings of flesh and bone (Luke 10:31–32). Nor are they called to selfishly accumulate things thinking that one's life "consist[s] in the abundance of possessions" (Luke 12:15). Consequently, they should individually and collectively be like their Lord and Master, "a friend of tax collectors and sinners" (Luke 7:34), proclaiming the goods news of the kingdom of God everyday in cities and villages (Luke 8:1). According to Luke no other missional path exists. As Jesus indicated in the synagogue of Nazareth, compelled by the power of the Holy Spirit, we are called "*to proclaim the year of the Lord's favor*" (Luke 4:19) in our particular historical context. This is how it must be. We do not have another alternative.

2

The Galilean Option of Jesus

Mission from the Periphery of the World

INTRODUCTION

God's special love for the poor and the marginalized is a central theme that holds together the liberating message of the Bible. The biblical perspective is conclusive. The Old and New Testament underscore that God is particularly concerned with the insignificant in history, the defenseless and needy, the fragile and scorned, the underprivileged, and the excluded and the weak of this world. God is their *goël* or their defender, redeemer, liberator, and protector. One cannot deny or hide the biblical evidence, especially the call given to the people of God to defend the cause of the poor, practicing justice and asserting what is right, for only in this way can one be a friend of God, the author of life. In this sense, not practicing justice and perverting what is right constitutes turning one's back on God's purpose and opting for the way of death.

One of the essential components of the liberating mission of Jesus of Nazareth, the traveling preacher from Galilee, was inverting the destiny of the poor and the marginalized, radically transforming social and economic relations contrary to the principles of the kingdom of God.[1] One of the New Testament documents that emphasizes this key biblical theme is the gospel of Luke. Luke repeatedly highlights God's special love for the poor and the rejected, the "scum" of society, and those on the other bank of history and the high tide of exclusion.[2] According to the Lucan account, during his missionary journey through cities and villages (Luke 8:1), Jesus of Nazareth publicly proclaimed that he had come to announce good news to the poor. He declared this from the very beginning of his traveling ministry, when on a day of rest in a synagogue in Nazareth he expounded his messianic platform, also called the programmatic discourse (Luke 4:16–30). The Lucan theological perspective is extremely clear: from the world of the poor an integral view of mission which seeks the transformation of all things is weaved, radical discipleship marked by an unshakeable faith in the God of life is articulated, the nonnegotiable value of life as a gift of God is affirmed, peace is built, and the dignity of all human beings as created by God is asserted. In this way, Luke expands the missionary horizon, opening it to new situations, and the reach of the liberating mission of the carpenter from Nazareth is extended. The Galilean Option of Jesus becomes a serious commitment, a profound calling that sinks its roots into the world of the poor, an inescapable pilgrimage, and an inevitable route marked out by the cross and the hope of the resurrection. In his gospel Luke shows us the path to follow; he summons us to a radical discipleship marked by provocative missional positions, gestures of solidarity, programmatic realizations, and permanent jubilees. For Luke, doing mission from the periphery of the world has its risks and necessary cost, for it deals with an adventure of faith

---

1. Hertig, "Jubilee Mission of Jesus," 167–79.

2. Luke also emphasizes other key themes. One of theme is the theme of *prayer* (Luke 3:2; 5:16; 6:12; 9:18, 29; 11:1–3; 18:1–8, 9–14; 22:32; 23:40). The Holy Spirit is another recurring theme in this gospel (Luke 1:15, 35, 41, 67; 2:25–27; 3:16, 22; 4:1, 14, 18). Luke also stresses the universality of salvation (Luke 2:32; 3:6; 4:16–30; 24:45–49). The theme of joy is also present as another distinguishing characteristic of the gospel (Luke 1.44, 58; 2:10, 20; 24:41, 52–53), and the same can be said of discipleship (Luke 5:1–11; 9:57–62; 14:25–35). And an understanding of the day of rest as an opportune occasion to affirm human dignity and as an appropriate time to celebrate life is another central theme in this gospel (Luke 6:6–11; 13:10–17; 14:1–6).

nourished by hope, an urgent calling whose contents are connected with a non-negotiable commitment to life.

WHY GALILEE?

"Can anything good come out of Nazareth?" (John 1:46). "Surely you are not also from Galilee, are you? Search and you will see that no prophet is to arise from Galilee" (John 7:52). Both questions, assertions recorded only by John in his gospel, express the opinion that the Jews from Jerusalem had toward this obscure province of first century Palestine. Galilee was considered in this time as

> an unimportant region of the country. All but ignored in the Old Testament, it is called "The District of the Gentiles" in Isaiah 8:23 (a text cited in Mt 4:15–16); the Gospels, however, will speak of it often. It was a region looked down upon by the inhabitants of Judea, where Jerusalem was located. Galilee was a provincial area, close to pagan populations, which influenced its speech and distinctive accent . . . , its customs, and its quite unorthodox religious practices. Nothing good could come from Galilee: of this all good Jews were convinced.[3]

The situation of poverty and marginality in Galilee contrasted notably with the privileges Jerusalem enjoyed as the religious, political, cultural, and economic center of Palestine. The difference between Galilee and Jerusalem was abysmal. While Galilee was synonymous with extreme poverty, shame, and marginalization, Jerusalem enjoyed a set of privileges that further deepened the differences. This explains why the Jews of Jerusalem scornfully treated the uncultured and ragged Galileans, as can be deduced from the reference recorded by Luke in Acts: "uneducated and ordinary men" (Acts 4:13). An author summarizes the contrast that existed between Galilee and Jerusalem as follows:

> During the ministry of Jesus there was in Galilee a group of disinherited people without a country. This was the product of immigration from Judah in search for better living conditions. It is likely, due to the possibilities and opportunities in Galilee, that it became overpopulated. There was an abundance of orphans, widows, poor, and unemployed.

---

3. Gutiérrez, *God of Life*, 99.

> This situation was a contrast to the kind of life Jews were liv-
> ing in Jerusalem. Things were different there. The mere fact that
> Jerusalem was the religious centre gave her and her inhabitants
> a privileged existence.[4]

This impoverished and spurned province, inhabited by multitudes of
poor who were in a situation of death, was the place Jesus chose to begin
his traveling ministry through towns and villages. The synoptic gospels
unanimously record that from the obscure region of Galilee Jesus began
to preach the good news of the kingdom of God (Matt 4:12–17; Mark
1:14–15; Luke 4:14–21). Mark underlines this in his gospel in this way:
"Now after John was arrested, Jesus came to Galilee, proclaiming the good
news of God, and saying, 'The time is fulfilled, and the kingdom of God
has come near; repent, and believe in the good news'" (Mark 1:14–15).

Matthew 4:12–25, a text parallel to Luke 4:16–30, is a key section
for understanding the liberating mission of Jesus. When it tells of the
start of Jesus' ministry in Galilee making use of a passage taken from
the prophet Isaiah, it says the following: ". . . Galilee of the Gentiles—the
people who sat in darkness have seen a great light, and for those who sat
in the region and shadow of death light has dawned" (Matt 4:15–16).
From this region that was seated in darkness and in the shadow of death,
Jesus of Nazareth began to proclaim the good news of liberation (Matt
4:17, 23).[5] The *kairos* or crucial time announced by the prophets of the
Old Testament had begun!

Luke records that on a day of rest in a synagogue in Nazareth, Jesus
expounded his messianic platform (Luke 4:16–30), whose connection
to the year of jubilee cannot be denied (Lev 25:1–55). The content and
reach of the messianic platform expounded in the synagogue of Nazareth
explain why it is constantly underlined in the accounts of the third gospel
that the liberating mission of Jesus aims to reverse the destiny of the poor
and the marginalized. According to Luke, Jesus of Nazareth fulfilled the
expectations of the Old Testament in his person and ministry. Indeed,
in addition to Luke, the other synoptic gospels clearly express that the

---

4. Saracco, "Liberating Options of Jesus," 34.

5. Paul Hertig holds that in Matthew's gospel the term Galilee is emphasized more
than in the other gospels. He affirms that, "Matthew introduces and concludes the ministry of Jesus in Galilee." He proposes that Galilee is a missiological key that indicates
that God accepts those excluded by society and commissions them to be agents of
change in the world ("Galilee Theme in Matthew," 155).

kingdom of God had come near in Jesus of Nazareth (Matt 4:17; Mark 1:15) and that a concrete sign of this was that the good news was announced to the poor (Luke 4:18; 6:20; 7:22). In light of all of this information, it is clear that from the periphery of the world, from the corner of the dead, from spurned Galilee the proclamation of the kingdom began. As Luke clearly indicates in his gospel, from the home of the disinherited and the ragged of the world, Jesus began his liberating mission. Was Jesus' choice of Galilee circumstantial? No. The Galilean Option of Jesus was not circumstantial. In the words of Padilla:

> A good portion of Jesus' ministry unfolded in the underdeveloped province of Galilee. Galilee, to the north of Palestine, was an abandoned region. Jesus' ministry was concentrated in this impoverished sector of the Jewish nation of his time. . . . Why? Why did he not carry out his ministry mainly in Judea and in Jerusalem? In Jerusalem he could have had access to the political and religious power of his time, and who knows, he could have had some influence in the handling of the region's affairs. Perhaps his message could have been disseminated with greater efficiency. But no, he opted for Galilee. . . . I would like to suggest that this is not circumstantial, that Jesus' choice of this underdeveloped region of Palestine was an intentional option. In effect, it was an option for the poor. . . . Jesus opted for Galilee because there he was going to carry out his ministry among the masses forgotten by the leaders. . . .[6]

The Galilean Option of Jesus was neither incidental nor circumstantial. The synoptic gospels testify that he intentionally opted for Galilee, that spurned and marginalized region inhabited principally by the poor and excluded. Jesus began his missionary pilgrimage in Galilee (Matt 4:12–23; Mark 1:14–15; Luke 4:16–21). At the shores of the Sea of Galilee he called his first disciples (Matt 4:18–25; Mark 1:16–20). After his resurrection he appeared to his disciples in Galilee (Matt 28:16; Mark 16:6–7) and there he gave them the missionary task of making disciples of every nation (Matt 28:16–20). It remains clear, then, that the Galilean Option of Jesus was an intentional option that took into account his special concern for the poor and the marginalized. This radical option provoked continual disagreements with the representatives of the established religion that did not tolerate listening to the voice of the insignificant, to the proposition

6. Padilla, "La Opción Galilea," 1, 6.

of integral liberation that came from scorned Galilee, or to the good news of the kingdom of God proclaimed by a humble carpenter from Nazareth (Matt 13:55; Mark 6:3; Luke 4:22).

Jesus' Galilean Option shows that from solidarity with the weak, from whole-hearted identification with those who suffer, from an unwavering commitment to the scorned, from the poor of the earth, he began to declare the good news of the kingdom of God. Luke, in Acts, records that Jesus presented himself as Jesus of Nazareth (Acts 22:8) and that the apostolic church did not hide this fact in its preaching and testimony (Acts 4:10). Consequently, taking into account the Lucan testimony, it can be affirmed that the Galilean Option consists of joyful life and underlying danger of death, suffering and hope, fidelity and obedience, renunciation and voluntary surrender. The cross and the resurrection form the backbone of Christian commitment to the poor and the marginalized of the world.

Four theological themes or key thematic axes, which are connected to one another, are central to Jesus' Galilean Option. Each one of these themes has specific connotations that contribute to outline the proposal of Jesus' Galilean Option. The messianic platform articulates the point of departure, especially since, in the programmatic discourse of Nazareth, Jesus lays out both the nature and reach of his liberating mission. The content of the message, the good news of the kingdom of God, constitutes the second key theological theme of Jesus' Galilean Option. The recipients of the good news of the kingdom of God is another one of the key theological themes upon which the Galilean Option is built. The recipients are both objects of God's special love and active subjects in the task of communicating the good news of liberation. The fourth theme is an understanding of discipleship as a permanent commitment that ultimately aims to construct a new society or alternative community based on the essential principles of the kingdom of God.

THE MESSIANIC MANIFESTO OF NAZARETH

Luke 4:16–30 is a key text that clearly outlines Jesus' understanding of his mission and that is considered as the foundation of the entire gospel of Luke and as a prelude to Acts.[7] It outlines the messianic program, manifesto, and platform of Jesus. It fulfills the same function as Acts 1:8, as it

---

7. Ford, "Reconciliation and Forgiveness," 83.

acts as a summary of the entire gospel, which Luke continues to amplify as he records acts that show the liberating mission of Jesus. In this sense, each Lucan account intends to illustrate with concrete and paradigmatic cases the reaches of the jubilee announced by Jesus in the synagogue of Nazareth. Therefore, the preference the Lucan Jesus has for the excluded and the "nobodies" of the society of his time is not merely incidental. It is not incidental precisely because the messianic platform expounded in the synagogue of Nazareth indicates that the liberating mission of Jesus aimed to invert the destiny of the poor and the marginalized. What are the contents and specific reach of Jesus' messianic platform or program-matic discourse in the synagogue of Nazareth? Luke describes this scene and the words of Jesus on this occasion in this way:

> When he came to Nazareth, where he had been brought up, he went to the synagogue on the sabbath day, as was his custom. He stood up to read, and the scroll of the prophet Isaiah was given to him. He unrolled the scroll and found the place where it was writ-ten: "The Spirit of the Lord is upon me, because he has anointed me to bring good news to the poor. He has sent me to proclaim release to the captives and recovery of sight to the blind, to let the oppressed go free, to proclaim the year of the Lord's favor." And he rolled up the scroll, gave it back to the attendant, and sat down. The eyes of all in the synagogue were fixed on him. Then he began to say to them, "Today this scripture has been fulfilled in your hearing" (Luke 4:16–21).[8]

Opinions regarding this key text of the third gospel vary depending on both on the ecclesiastical tradition and theological objective of the specialists in sacred Scripture. Thus, for example, for Gustavo Gutiérrez:

> Jesus, making use of a text of the prophet Isaiah (61:1–2; 58:6), publicly explains his program. It is about a text that fulfills in the gospel of Luke a function similar to that of Exodus in the Old Testament. Both express the liberating will of God. . . . Luke uses the scene of the visit to Nazareth . . . to tell us what the messianic

---

8. The messianic manifesto of Nazareth does not culminate in Luke 4:21, as for a greater understanding of its contents and specific missionary reaches, one must con-sider Luke 4:16–30 as a single block with the entire Lucan account as a backdrop. It is understood in this way, for example, by John Howard Yoder (*Politics of Jesus*, 34) and Beda Rigaux (*Historia de Jesús*, 111–13, 273).

work consisted of, and he takes great care to make sure we see its universal reach.[9]

Alejandro Cussianovich follows along the same interpretative line as Gustavo Gutiérrez and points out that the task of the Messiah consists of giving "concrete social embodiment to the Lord's year of favor."[10] John Howard Yoder, meanwhile, holds that, "Here the passage from Isaiah 61 which Jesus turns upon himself is not only a most explicitly messianic one: it is one which states the messianic expectation in the most expressly social terms."[11]

René Padilla has more specifically explained the concrete missionary effect of the programmatic manifesto of Nazareth, pointing out that:

> Right at the beginning of his ministry, in the manifesto on his mission he presented in the synagogue of Nazareth, he read the prophetic pronouncement in Isaiah 61:1–2 and went on to claim that he who would fulfill it had arrived. The fact that he applied that passage to himself makes it obvious that Jesus understood his mission in terms of the inauguration of a new era—"the day of the Lord's favor"—marked by the proclamation of good news to the poor, release for the captives, sight for the blind, and liberty for the oppressed. Seen in the light of the Old Testament background, Jesus' view of his mission implies that he, as the Messiah, is bringing in "the acceptable year of the Lord"—that is, the year of jubilee, of the structuring of society according to the demands of justice and love. He is the bearer of the blessings of the Kingdom, and these blessings will be released among people living in conditions of deprivation and oppression, poverty and exploitation.[12]

Paul Hertig, in an interesting analysis of the messianic manifesto of Nazareth that situates this key text of Luke's gospel in its specific theological context, states that it is necessary to take into account two very significant facts.[13] First, when Jesus cites Isa 61:1–2, he intentionally does not read the last part of Isa 61:2 ("and the day of vengeance of our God"). Hertig holds that this indicates that Jesus avoided any reference of hostility

---

9. Gutiérrez, "Primera Declaración Mesiánica," 6–7, my translation.

10. Cussianovich, *Religious Life and the Poor*, 158.

11. Yoder, *Politics of Jesus*, 34–35.

12. Padilla, *Mission Between the Times*, 175.

13. Hertig, "Jubilee Mission of Jesus," 167–79.

toward the Gentiles. In other words, Jesus proclaimed the impartial grace of God, which is also underlined in the reference in Luke 4:25–27 to two Gentiles who received God's favor, the widow of Zarephath and Naaman the Syrian. Second, in Luke 4:18, a phrase taken from Isa 58:6 is inserted ("to let the oppressed go free"). This text of the prophet Isaiah, if examined in light of the whole underlying proposition of Isaiah 58, in which hypocritical and superficial religious practices are denounced and it is emphasized that the true fast consists of breaking the chains of injustice and being concerned with the situation of the poor, has an undeniable social dimension and acts as a corrective for a religion unconcerned with the concrete material conditions that the oppressed live in.

Luke 4:16–30 is, then, a text key to capturing the theological richness and the concrete reaches of the Lucan proposition. It emphasizes both the universal reach of the liberating mission of Jesus and his special love for the poor and the marginalized. This is so because in his programmatic discourse expounded in the synagogue of Nazareth, Jesus clearly established that non-Jews were also recipients of the good news of the impartial love of God. This is likewise confirmed by the intentional omission of the final part of Isa 61:2 and the reference to the widow of Zarephath and Naaman the Syrian. Moreover, since the word *ptōchos* (poor) is used in Luke 4:18, it has the connotation of material need, deprivation, and misery.[14] Even more, the brokenhearted,[15] the captives, and the blind mentioned in Luke 4:18 also express concrete forms of deprivation and material poverty. These two themes, the universality of mission and the special love for the poor and the marginalized, form the pillars that support the messianic platform expounded in the synagogue of Nazareth. They are also two inescapable, urgent, and non-negotiable agenda items for the mission of the church. Faithfulness to all of God's counsel demands that in all understanding of Jesus' Galilean Option and of the consequences that this option has for the mission of the church on all political, social, and cultural frontiers, these two non-negotiable items of the good news of the kingdom of God should not be absent.

---

14. The word *ptōchos* is used ten times in the gospel of Luke (4:19; 6:20; 7:22; 14:13, 21; 16:20, 22; 18:22; 19:8; 21:1) to designate all who find themselves in a situation of extreme poverty and are compelled to beg.

15. See KJV.

THE CONTENT OF THE LIBERATING MESSAGE

In his gospel Luke emphasizes that the good news that Jesus of Nazareth began to proclaim from the marginal and scorned region of Galilee, in which nearly ninety percent of Jews could be classified as poor,[16] was the eruption of the kingdom of God on the stage of history. In various moments the Lucan account emphasizes the centrality of this message. Only on two occasions does Luke use the phrase "good news of the kingdom of God" (Luke 4:43; 8:1). In other instances he simply uses the word kingdom (Luke 11:2; 12:32; 22:29, 30; 23.42). In the majority of cases he employs the phrase *basileía to theou* or kingdom of God (Luke 6:20; 7:28; 8:10; 9:2, 11, 27, 60, 62; 10:9, 11; 11:20; 12:31; 13:18, 20, 28, 29; 14:15; 16:16; 17:20 [2], 21; 18:16, 17, 24, 25, 29 19:11; 21:31 22:16, 18). Although the terminology is not the same, what is clear in all of the cases is that the content of the message that Jesus proclaimed was derived fundamentally from the specific meaning of the word kingdom or *basileia*, and in his person and ministry the promises of the Old Testament pertaining to the Messiah were being fulfilled. Luke clearly establishes that the kingdom of God had come near and that Jesus of Nazareth is the self-*basileia*, since in him and through him God has inserted himself into history or has contextualized himself in Jesus Christ.[17] Or, as one author has precisely stated: "Jesus is not merely the preacher of the Kingdom, He is at the same time the bearer and fulfiller of it. . . . The Gospel is not only the message *of* Jesus but the message about the person of Jesus. That is why entrance into the Kingdom is entirely governed by faith."[18]

What is emphasized here is the present aspect or dimension of the kingdom of God. In accordance with the Lucan language, the marrow of the message of Jesus of Nazareth was the announcement of the eruption of the kingdom among us. But this is not all that Luke details in his gospel, as in various sections he refers to both the present and future dimensions of the kingdom. In the words of Fitzmyer:

> In the Lucan Gospel, however, Jesus is the kingdom-preacher par excellence. . . . The first proclamation of [the kingdom of God] in the Lucan Gospel is made by Jesus (4:43), even though Luke has omitted any reference to it in his parallel to the first dramatic

---

16. Hertig, "Jubilee Mission of Jesus," 172.

17. Padilla, "Evangelio de los Pobres," 43.

18. Roux, "Kingdom," 219.

announcement of it in Mark 1:15. . . . When the first proclamation of the kingdom of God is made in Luke (4:43), Jesus is there
made to add significantly, "That is what I was sent for!" . . . There
is, moreover, a sense in which the Lucan Jesus speaks of the im-
minence of the kingdom: "Realize that the kingdom of God is
near" (21:31; see also 10:11). Yet he does not hesitate to speak of
its presence in his own person and acts, "The kingdom of God
is among you" (17:21 . . .). Furthermore, he can also speak of
certain things being fulfilled in the coming kingdom (22:16, 30).
We note here that these specifically Lucan passages dealing with
the kingdom have a two-pronged reference, to a present and a
future aspect of it – a reference that is not without its significance for the eschatology of the Lucan writings.[19]

The *already* and *not yet* of the kingdom, the eschatological tension,
is present then in the Lucan testimony. However, it is also necessary to
point out that the reference to the kingdom of God and its eruption into
history involves the usage of concrete social and political language that
had a defined and precise connotation in the Jewish mentality of the first
century. According to Yoder:

The language, "kingdom," "evangel," is chosen from the political
realm. This particular selectivity of vocabulary would be most
out of place if Jesus' whole point had been that over against the
expectations of John, he was not interested in this realm. It hard-
ly needs to be argued that "kingdom" is a political term; the common Bible reader is less aware that "gospel" as well means not
just any old welcome report but the kind of publicly important
proclamation that is worth sending with a runner and holding a
celebration when it is received.[20]

Yoder's valuable observation reveals an important fact. One cannot
"spiritualize" the social and political content precisely because the word
kingdom is employed, nor can one neglect the transforming effect derived from that content. Doing so would be a negation both of the message of the gospel and of its integrally liberating power. In this sense the
proclamation of the good news of the kingdom of God always provokes
"theological crises," successive conversions, and radical repentances that
challenge us to depend on God's grace at every moment, rather than on

19. Fitzmyer, *Gospel According to Luke*, 154–55.

20. Yoder, *Politics of Jesus*, 34.

the reductionist or idealist theology that is in fashion that has converted the gospel into a cheap commodity subject to the law of supply and demand. Disciples who are faithful and obedient to the charge of Jesus of Nazareth must understand that proclaiming and living the reign of God involves entering openly and frontally into conflict with the "prince of this age" and his agents. In spite of this reality, they must joyfully assume the cost of following Jesus and the Galilean Option, which is the correlate to this following, as a pilgrimage founded in an unbreakable faith in the God of life. The God of life sends us to the world to be ambassadors of life, artisans of peace, and preachers of his justice. Consequently, we cannot deny that God's purpose is the complete restructuring of all of creation, which of course includes a radical inversion of the pyramid of power and the concrete task of reversing the destiny of the poor and the marginalized. The mission of the church is closely connected with the announcement of the kingdom of God, an announcement that becomes concrete in the individual and public testimony of the disciples of the crucified and risen Jesus of Nazareth, disciples that are open to offering their lives before denying their faith or conforming to the predominant society.

THE RECIPIENTS OF THE GOOD NEWS OF THE KINGDOM

Who are the recipients of the good news of salvation? In a full sense, according to Luke, all human beings are. It has already been pointed out that one of the Lucan emphases is the universality of mission. This implies that all human beings, poor and rich, male and female, are recipients of the good news of salvation. Clear indicatives of this reality include, for example, the theological intention underlined in the genealogy of Jesus recorded by Luke that lists the ancestors of the Messiah back to Adam (Luke 3:23–38) and the song of the aged Simeon, in which he states that the advent of the Messiah would be "a light for revelation to the Gentiles" (Luke 2:32). The same idea is present in the accounts of the healing of the centurion's servant (Luke 7:1–10), the parable of the Good Samaritan (Luke 10:25–37), the healing of the Samaritan who suffered from leprosy (Luke 17:11–19), the mention of the queen of the South who came to listen to the wisdom of Solomon (Luke 11:31), the reference to the inhabitants of Nineveh who repented when Jonah preached about God's impending judgment on that place (11:32), and the final commission that the good news of repentance and forgiveness of sins be preached in all nations (Luke 24:47). This also seems to be the central idea of the parable of the great banquet (Luke 14:15–24).

Moreover, in his gospel Luke insistently underlines that Jesus had a special love or special preference for the poor and the marginalized. The evidence that exists in the third gospel regarding this special love for the dispossessed and underprivileged cannot be pushed aside or ignored. Beyond the fact that Luke is particularly sensitive to social realities, what is emphasized in the third gospel is that the God of life takes particular interest in the situation of oppression in which the fragile and needy of society find themselves. Luke underlines that Jesus of Nazareth "lost face" for them, valuing and treating them as human beings created in the image of God. The social sectors condemned to the garbage dump of history are from the Lucan perspective the privileged recipients of and active subjects in the communication of the good news of liberation. The Lucan Jesus is recurrently in contact with the peripheral groups of his time and carries out his ministry travelling through towns and villages (Luke 8:1; 13:22) of the spurned region of Galilee, moving through all sectors of society, especially among the poor and marginalized. From Marshall's perspective: "No one can fail to observe that Luke shows particularly how Jesus brought salvation to the less privileged people in Judea—the poor, women, children and notorious sinners—and how, although for the most part he confined his ministry to the Jews, he indicated plainly that the gospel embraced the Gentiles, and in particular the despised Samaritans."[21]

In his gospel Luke highlights the central role that the forgotten of the earth had in the happenings he records. The Lucan Jesus sits at the table with them (Luke 5:27–32; 8:36–50), touches with his hands the untouchables like the lepers (Luke 5:12–16), incorporates as followers various Galilean women (Luke 8:2–3), relates with the vile and despicable like the Samaritan leper (Luke 17:11–19), becomes friends with public sinners like Zacchaeus, a chief tax collector (Luke 19:1–10), and has a special predilection for children, who were considered as incomplete human beings (Luke 9:46–48; 18:15–17). The Galilean Option of Jesus, in which the fragile and the scorned had a privileged place, is quite clear. During his missionary travels Jesus "befriends and shares table fellowship with tax collectors and sinners. . . . More than any other evangelist Luke emphasizes Jesus' association with women. . . . The Lucan Jesus is open to 'official' outsiders such as the Gentile centurion . . . and Samaritans. . . .

21. Marshall, "Luke," 887.

Jesus reaches out to lepers . . . and care for the poor is a constant theme of his preaching."[22]

Luke is the gospel for the exiles of the earth who do not count for anything, for the needy and the marginalized of the world, for the defenseless and the ragged of society. From the moment Jesus began his ministry as a traveling preacher in the scorned province of Galilee to the moment he set his face toward Jerusalem (Luke 9:51), they were the center of his special preference. According to Luke's gospel, he related with marginalized social sectors like women (Luke 7:3–50; 8:2–3, 43–48; 10:38–42; 13:10–17; 21:1–4; 23:25; 24:10, 22–24), lepers (Luke 5:12–16; 17:11–19), publicans (Luke 5:27–32; 15:1; 19:1–10), Samaritans (Luke 17:16), children (Luke 9:47; 18:15–17) and the sick (Luke 4:40; 5:17–26; 6:6–11, 17–19; 7:1–10, 21; 13:10–17; 18:35–43). He used them as examples of openness to God (Luke 7:43–48; 17:16–19) and demanded that others be like them (Luke 18:15–17). In his parables he placed them as examples to be followed (Luke 10:25–37; 18:9–14), contrasting their spiritual sensitivity with the hypocrisy of the scribes and Pharisees. In addition, he risked being accused of being "a glutton and drunkard, a friend of tax collectors and sinners" (Luke 7:34), of violating the day of rest (Luke 6:7; 14:1–6), and of associating with the scum of society (Luke 5:30; 19:7). The Lucan Jesus understood who the men of his time were marginalizing, scorning, or treating as human waste or disposable articles.[23] All of these sectors confined to social ostracism, treated as useless, and condemned to silence were the privileged recipients of the good news of liberation. When the poor and the marginalized encountered Jesus, they affirmed their human dignity and passed from death to life. Jesus humanized them, defying the dehumanizing cultural patterns of his time. Each one of these scorned and underprivileged, excluded and needy, passed from isolation to community and from orphanhood to comradeship when they encountered him.

---

22. Senior and Stuhlmueller, *Biblical Foundations for Mission*, 261.

23. In relation to this Gustavo Gutiérrez points out that: "In the cultural world of Judaism at that time, children were regarded as incomplete human beings; along with the poor, the sick, and women, they were counted among the unimportant folk (*God of Life*, 114). He further states that, "Those who suffered from some serious illness or some bodily deformity were regarded as sinners (see John 9). This is why lepers, for example, were cut off from the life of society. . . . On the other hand, public sinners, such as tax collectors and prostitutes, were also regarded as the scum of society" (*God of Life*, 115).

THE PATH OF DISCIPLESHIP

The gospel of Luke contains three fundamental passages that outline the marks and radicalism of discipleship (Luke 5:1–11; 9:57–62; 14:25–35). From the Lucan perspective, being a disciple of Christ does not prove to be easy. The price is extremely high and the demands are raised. The shortcuts are not valid. Discipleship is a calling that demands voluntary surrender and incites urgent commitments. This is clear in the following exclusively Lucan passage.

> Now large crowds were traveling with him; and he turned and said to them, "Whoever comes to me and does not hate father and mother, wife and children, brothers and sisters, yes, and even life itself, cannot be my disciple. Whoever does not carry the cross and follow me cannot be my disciple. . . . So therefore, none of you can become my disciple if you do not give up all your possessions" (Luke 14:25–27, 33).

Discipleship entails a complete restructuring of life, an epistemological conversion, and a radical change in values that demands obedience and firm decisions. In other words, once one has made the decision to follow Jesus, there is no turning back. Thus the gospel indicates: "No one who puts a hand to the plow and looks back is fit for the kingdom of God" (Luke 9:62). Jesus is the one who chooses his disciples, challenging them to follow him and giving them specific tasks (Luke 5:10–11, 27–32; 6:12–13; 9:1–6; 10:1–12). In this way he introduces what Yoder has called a "community of voluntary commitment."

> The point is rather that in a society characterized by very stable, religiously undergirded family ties, Jesus is here calling into being a community of voluntary commitment, willing for the sake of its calling to take upon itself the hostility of the given society. . . . What matters is the quality of the life to which the disciple is called. The answer is that to be a disciple is to share in that style of life of which the cross is the culmination. . . .
>
> There are thus about the community of disciples those sociological traits most characteristic of those who set about to change society: a visible structured fellowship, a sober decision guaranteeing that the costs of commitment to the fellowship have been consciously accepted, and a clearly defined lifestyle distinct from that of the crowd.[24]

24. Yoder, *Politics of Jesus*, 45–47.

The disciple is someone who has passed from death to life, inserting himself or herself into a concrete community of human beings of flesh and bone, where solidarity is a distinctive mark and love is a concrete gesture. The new humanity, the community of the King, is present in history, and the disciples are a visible sign of this new reality.

Luke emphasizes that a disciple of Jesus is the one who follows him, having consciously accepted his invitation, and for this reason is unable to turn back. His or her mission is a continuation of the mission of the carpenter from Nazareth. He or she has the cross as an unconcealed sign of his or her commitment, thus sharing in the life, the destiny, and the dignity of his or her Lord.[25] In other words, from the Lucan perspective, discipleship has as its point of departure a definitive encounter with the Lord of life on the stage of history. It is about an encounter that recreates us by means of a profound and radical repentance that incorporates us into the community of Jesus. From this moment the disciple has an obligatory commitment to be an ambassador of the kingdom, a passionate defender of life, a maker of justice, and an artisan of peace. The cross is the unmistakable sign that the disciple belongs to the kingdom, having the hope of resurrection as an unshakeable foundation and the table of the kingdom as the supreme goal that invigorates obedient testimony every day. In the words of Dietrich Bonhoeffer:

> Such grace is *costly* because it calls us to follow, and it is *grace* because it calls us to follow *Jesus Christ*. It is costly because it costs a man his life, and it is grace because it gives a man the only true life. . . . It is *costly* because it cost God the life of his Son: "ye were bought at a price," and what has cost God much cannot be cheap for us. Above all, it is *grace* because God did not reckon his Son too dear a price to pay for our life, but delivered him up for us. Costly grace is the Incarnation of God.[26]

Surrender is essential to discipleship. There can be no following without a cross, without voluntary surrender because of his grace. Surrender and obedience walk together on the *via crucis* of discipleship. The Lucan testimony explains that at the feet of the cross, under the glorious dawn of the resurrection, definitive callings, encounters that mark history, and decisions aimed at the table of the kingdom are found. As

25. Ryan, "Women from Galilee," 56.
26. Bonhoeffer, *Cost of Discipleship*, 47–48.

Orlando Costas has pointed out: "Obedience to Jesus is at the same time the prelude to and the test of true discipleship."[27]

As it occurred many years ago with several of the first disciples, when we are at our daily work casting the net into the sea (Matt 4:18) or mending the nets (Matt 4:21), Jesus comes to us. And when he says, "Follow me," he awaits definitive responses. Hesitations, double-mindedness, Phariseeisms, and cheap religiosity are left behind. The Galilean Option is a way that opens an expectant track marked out by promises and transformed lives that have placed their eyes on the present and future of God. Luke clears the way to understanding both the content of and the radical consequences of discipleship. According to Fitzmyer:

> To be a disciple of Christ one has to follow him along the road that he walks to his destiny in Jerusalem, his *exodos*, his transit to the Father. . . .
>
> Thus for Luke Christian discipleship is portrayed not only as the acceptance of a master's teaching, but as the identification of oneself with the master's way of life and destiny in an intimate, personal following of him. Because of the geographical perspective in the Gospel, the "following" has a pronounced spatial nuance: the disciple must walk in the footsteps of Jesus.[28]

Jesus still continues saying, "*Akolouthei moi* (Follow me)" (Luke 5:27; 9:59; 18:22). The route that one should follow goes from Galilee to Jerusalem, from the periphery to the center of power. The cross is the way of life, obedience that hatches liberating joy, loyalty that is tested on the way to glory. Discipleship is possible because life has won. In the Galilean Option, cross and resurrection mark the way to "the city that has foundations, whose architect and builder is God" (Heb 11:10). Disciples are called to participate in the mission of Jesus. The road from Galilee to Jerusalem awaits us today as it did yesterday. On this journey it should never be forgotten that "discipleship means joy."[29]

27. Costas, "Misión como Discipulado," 55, my translation. *Contextual Theology for Latin America,* ed. Sharon E. Heaney, 219.

28. Fitzmyer, *Gospel According to Luke,* 241.

29. Bonhoeffer, *Cost of Discipleship,* 41.

3

The Path of Discipleship

From Marginalization to Comradeship

Luke 5:27–32

INTRODUCTION

The marginalization of persons and of specific human sectors was a recurring social phenomenon in the historical reality in which Jesus of Nazareth, traveling through towns and villages, proclaimed the good news of the kingdom of God (Luke 8:1; cf. Matt. 4:23; 9:35). Part of this problem is reflected in the way publicans or tax collectors were treated. In the cultural world of the first century, tax collectors, Jewish or pagan, formed part of the social sectors scorned and marginalized by Jews.[1] The strictest Jews considered them as religiously impure due to their constant relations with Gentiles and commonly associated them with other sinners like women of bad reputation in order to underline their position in

1. Ford, "Reconciliation and Forgiveness," 83.

the lowest stratum of society (Matt 11:19; 21:31–32; Mark 2:15–16; Luke 7:34; 15.1). Gooding points out that publicans were condemned to social ostracism[2] and Cole emphasizes their condition as outcasts of Jewish society.[3] The Jews hated and rejected publicans, treating them as social trash, especially because they extorted and committed fraud against their compatriots.[4] John the Baptist's public denunciation, "Collect no more than the amount prescribed for you" (Luke 3:13), and the words of Zaccheaus, the chief tax collector, "If I have defrauded anyone of anything, I will pay back four times as much" (Luke 19:8), are two clear indicators of this normal practice of publicans. The people despised such an occupation and considered them as sinners.[5] But the publicans were also socially marginalized. The Jews treated them as traitors and undesirable riffraff, because they collaborated with the Roman invaders by collecting taxes established by imperial authority.

It is powerfully attention-grabbing that, knowing firsthand the situation of social, cultural, and religious marginalization facing the tax collectors, Jesus connected himself with these undesirables (Luke 15:1–2; 19:1–10), and, even more, that he invited one of them to become part of the community of disciples (Luke 5:27–28, cf. Matt 9:9; Mark 2:14).[6] But this is not strange if one takes into account that, from the Lucan perspec-

2. Gooding, *According to Luke*, 109.

3. Cole, *Mark*, 123–24.

4. Joachim Gnilka describes the occupation and practice of tax collectors in the time of Jesus in this way: "The publicans had to collect the customs duties, that is, the irregular taxes levied especially on goods upon passing over the borders of the country. . . . In contrast to taxes, the customs duties collected were not going to end up in the imperial coffer, but in the coffer of the ruler of the country; in Galilee, thus, in the coffer of Herod Antipas. The collection of customs duties was not carried out by state functionaries, but by tenants (*publicani*). These leased the customs of a region determined by a sum of money fixed for the year. They could keep what they collected beyond the fixed amount. If they brought in less, they had to pay from their own pocket what was lacking in order to meet the stipulated amount. For the recovery of the money, they put to use those employed under them. Levi would be one of these. The pretense for abuse and debauchery was due to the complete indetermination that frequently existed regarding the amount to charge on goods. Ambitious publicans ambitiously took advantage of this lack of determination or fixation of the amount to charge" (*Evangelio Según San Marcos*, vol. I, 123–24, my translation).

5. Gnilka, *Evangelio Según San Marcos*, vol. I, 123.

6. Commenting on this topic, Joachim Gnilka observes the following: "The calling of a publican to discipleship anticipates the scandal that will come later on at the feast with the publicans" (*Evangelio Según San Marcos*, vol. I, 123, my translation).

tive, the liberating mission of Jesus has as one of its key axes a special love for the outcasts and for the scum of society. Levi or Matthew was one of these individuals considered as human waste, as a social exile, as someone insignificant. Regarding this, Bock points out that: "Jesus does not merely forgive sinners, he openly associates with them."[7] France holds that: "The difference between Jesus and the Pharisees lies in their conception of the will of God: for the Pharisees the first priority is obedience to regulations, for Jesus a mission to the people."[8] For Jesus, the lives and dignity of individuals like publicans mattered much more than religious, social, and cultural prejudices that erected concrete walls to separate human beings. During his missionary travels, he constantly had contact with those who had been pushed to the side and treated as the scum of society by the religious who considered themselves righteous and without sin, like the Pharisee of the parable (Luke 18:9–14).

One of the biblical texts that allows us to grasp the meaning and reaches of Jesus' special preference for those on the periphery of society is Luke 5:27–32. This passage, which narrates the calling of Levi or Matthew the publican to be a disciple of Jesus, an account that is also found with certain variations in the other synoptic gospels (Matt 9:9–13; Mark 2:13–17), contains theological principles and missional lines that are extremely valuable for a commitment to the defense of life. This is especially relevant in the contemporary globalized world. The exclusion of millions of human beings who find themselves in a condition of abject poverty and absolute orphanhood, due to the implementation of economic policies that undervalue human dignity, presents itself as one of the most critical social problems and most acute ethical dilemmas of today.

THE RELATIONSHIP BETWEEN GOING OUT AND SEEING

In his account Luke mentions that when Jesus went out he saw Levi or Matthew, a known tax collector marginalized by Jewish society, seated in his usual place of work (Luke 5:27) The scene is located in Capernaum,[9]

---

7. Bock, *Luke*, 107.

8. France, *Matthew*, 168.

9. Capernaum (Greek = *Kafarnaoum* = village of Nahum) was located on the shore of the Sea of Galilee to the northeast of Galilee, near a political border on the international road between Syria and Egypt, which explains why there was a military base there (Matt 8:5–13; Luke 7:1–10) as well as a customs post (Mark 2:14) (Hendriksen, *Luke*, 262–63, 578–79; Kane, "Capernaum," 175).

a place that had an influx of travelers, and therefore, there was a customs post there. The occupation of publican fit perfectly with the border town of Capernaum, as the authorities needed these characters in the border regions to collect the taxes established by the laws of the time. The gospel of Matthew mentions that "as Jesus was walking along, he saw a man" (Matt 9:9). The gospel of Mark points out that, "Jesus went out again beside the sea. . . . As he was walking along, he saw Levi" (Mark 2:13–14). All of this information indicates that the synoptic gospels unanimously record that Jesus had to go out, and passing through near the Sea of Galilee, he found Matthew immersed in his daily work as a tax collector. The difference in the synoptic accounts is that Matthew and Mark suggest that Jesus was passing through this place or near this place (*paragon*), however, Luke omits this expression, thereby suggesting that Jesus went in a deliberate or intentional manner to see this tax collector: "After this he went out and saw a tax collector named Levi (Luke 5:27). Even more, Luke uses a very emphatic verb (*theaomai*, cf. Luke 23:55) for the expression "to see" ("saw"), which indicates that it deals with a very profound and uncommon way of seeing, of an intentional seeing, of a seeing that sees beyond appearances or the surface of things. This implies that "Jesus discerned the character of Levi."[10]

However, this way of seeing has as a preliminary condition the act of going out, of walking, of passing through. This action is directly related to the way a person faces the world, that is, to their lifestyle. Jesus, before seeing and intentionally meeting with an excluded person like Levi, had to go out first. From where did he have to go out in order to see? First, he had to break free—which is a concrete action of going out—from all of the social schemes and predominant cultural prejudices of his time that objectified human beings like Levi the publican. In this sense, Jesus was not a religious spectator; he was not among those who observe the human drama from their comfortable position on a balcony without daring to get their feet dirty by committing themselves to defending the fragile and needy of society. Jesus was a man of the road. He was one of those for whom the concrete human being, the individual of flesh and bone, mattered much more than religious prejudices that distorted the purpose of God. John A. Mackay is the theologian who has explained in a pedagogical manner the substantial difference that exists between remaining

---

10. Ford, *My Enemy Is My Guest*, 71.

on the balcony as a simple spectator of events and taking on the road as a lifestyle marked by commitment. According to Mackay:

> The Balcony thus conceived is the classical standpoint, and so the symbol, of the perfect spectator, for whom life and the universe are permanent objects of study and contemplation. . . . By the Road I mean the place where life is tensely lived, where thought has its birth in conflict and concern, where choices are made and decisions are carried out. It is the place of action, of pilgrimage, of crusade, where concern is never absent from the wayfarer's heart. On the Road a goal is sought, dangers are faced, life is poured out.[11]

Jesus lived on the road. It was there that he met and called his disciples, and it was on that same route of public commitment to defending the dignity of all human beings as creations of God that he also related with many marginalized persons and outcasts of society, like the tax collector Levi. On the road he saw the publican Levi submerged in his marginal space. But he did not see him in accordance with the socially accepted cultural norms of the time, as an outcast or social scum, as someone undesirable. He saw him as a human being and beneficiary of the good news of liberation, as a recipient of his liberating mission that aimed to reverse the destiny of the marginalized, as someone who was excluded and needed to be included in the kingdom community.

The close relationship that exists between going out and seeing, passing through and knowing the historical context, has tremendous value both for its theological connotation and for its missionary and pastoral scope. Seeing means making the effort to understand what occurs in the mission environment and directly meeting with, without hesitations, the defenseless and destitute of the world; it demands expanding the theological horizon and stripping it of all prejudices; it indicates adopting a fuller vision of the concrete reality in which one is situated. But in order to see, it is first necessary to go outside of our narrow theological framework and political conceptions that do not permit us to encounter poverty face to face and to know firsthand the subhuman conditions in which the marginalized and undesirable of our time find themselves. These narrow theologies and political ideologies limit active participation in the urgent task of defending human dignity. As authentic seeing has commitment as

---

11. Mackay, *Preface to Christian Theology*, 29–30.

its correlate, it draws us out of indifference and inserts us into concrete actions of service to our neighbors.

The analysis of social or political events from a tranquil academic position or from the balcony, beyond being limited by its meager connection with reality and its unconcern for real human beings, cannot claim to be a xerox copy of what occurs in the historical present. Speaking from within, connected to critical experiences of human beings of flesh and bone, has the advantage of providing us with a more genuine picture—beyond the cold statistical charts or the opinion polls—of the problems that the marginalized have to face every day. In order to know the world of the marginalized of our time, we must first come out of the tunnel of indifference, leaving aside all of the prejudices that limit the establishment of more inclusive social relations. Missional practice, in order to be contextual, and therefore committed, must sink its roots into the temporal setting in which the marginalized experience their joys and sorrows, construct their dreams and hopes, fight for each day's bread, create new forms of social communication, and express their incorruptible faith in the God of life, defending the cause of the destitute and the needy.

HUMAN BEINGS OF FLESH AND BONE

Human beings are not anonymous bodies without specific identities or life histories, objects that can be manipulated, disposable pieces subject to the invisible hand of the market, figures to nourish cold statistical charts of institutions of the State or of organizations tied to international cooperation. All human beings, regardless of their social condition or cultural background, have personal history, family roots, a defined face, and concrete material and spiritual needs. Human beings considered as the social rubbish of this time are not merely street children, thieves, drug addicts, prostitutes, alcoholics, or those with AIDS. Each one of them is situated in a specific time frame that comes with its own particular set of social, cultural, and religious prejudices. This was the situation of Matthew the tax collector, who was considered as an outcast and social exile in first century Palestine. Nevertheless, according to the unanimous testimony of the synoptic gospels, this person marginalized by the Jewish society of his time had his own name (Matthew or Levi), a national identity (Jewish), a social space (publican), and known family ties (son of Alphaeus). Regarding this, Luke only indicates that Jesus "saw a tax collector named

Levi" (Luke 5:27). However, Matthew and Mark provide two pieces of information that underline the human nature and family ties of this marginalized person. Matthew stresses that Jesus "saw a man [*ánthropos*] called Matthew" (Matt 9:9) and Mark specifies that this man was "son of Alphaeus" (Mark 2:14). It is thus clear that the synoptic gospels recognize Matthew the publican as a human being of flesh and bone, with unique personal characteristics and specific family ties.

Luke and the other synoptic gospels record how Jesus, breaking with the predominant social categories of his time, saw, valued, and treated Matthew the publican as a human being of flesh and bone with real needs. He did not see, value, and treat him as his contemporaries did, as the scum of society or as an undesirable traitor, unworthy of being valued and treated as a human being. How would this hated and scorned publican feel when a Jew like Jesus valued and treated him—perhaps for the first time in his life—as a human being and not as social waste? Luke emphasizes that when Jesus invited him to follow him, with this public act, he was valuing and treating a hated and scorned publican as a human being created in the image of God and as a beneficiary of the good news of liberation that he proclaimed. With these actions, he went about fulfilling what had been proclaimed in the synagogue of Nazareth. Jesus had come to give good news to the poor and the marginalized, to preach the year of the Lord's favor, the jubilee (Luke 4:18–19). The same attitude and practice should characterize the individual and collective testimony of the disciples of Jesus of Nazareth of this time. They also must see, not things or statistics, but human beings who find themselves in real situations of oppression. All disciples involved in pastoral tasks, in service projects, and in social action, and connected to the world of the poor and the marginalized, must understand that they work with human beings of flesh and bone and not with disposable things. This is how it must be, because human beings—subjects and not objects—with whom we relate everyday also know how to think, have emotions, and have the capacity to make decisions, and have the resources to organize themselves and construct new alternatives of life.

CROSSING BORDERS

The missional task demands that we cross borders of every kind. This includes those barriers that can mean putting our honor into question or our physical security at risk. In his time, when he began to proclaim the good news of the kingdom of God, Jesus of Nazareth already had to face this problem. There was in that historical context a set of cultural, social, and religious prejudices that separated human beings. Thus, for example, Jews who considered themselves as decent could not have contact with public sinners like tax collectors, much less have them as part of their close circle of friends. In spite of these prejudices that the Jews accepted as normal and correct, Jesus, calling into question the predominant cultural patterns of his time, met Matthew the tax collector within his marginal space, "sitting at the tax booth" (Luke 5:27). In Luke's account of the calling of the tax collector Levi—a much more elaborate account than that of Matthew or Mark—he seems to suggest that Jesus deliberately approached the tax booth where he encountered Matthew, a disgraceful place of work according to the popular opinion of the time, to invite him to follow him.[12] In other words, Jesus' action was not circumstantial or incidental; it was an intentional action that aimed to clearly establish that the kingdom community had to be an inclusive community. In this kingdom community, radically distinct from the predominant society of the time or any other society based on simple human presuppositions, the marginalized like Matthew the publican had a reserved spot. This is so because Luke, when he tells of the calling of Matthew the publican, shows that the marginalized were also recipients of the good news of liberation that Jesus proclaimed.

Like Matthew the publican, the marginalized and the destitute of today are not disconnected from the historical reality that they are situated in as human beings of flesh and bone. This is one of the principal reasons that the disciples of Jesus of Nazareth had to cross all kinds of borders in order to know firsthand the specific needs of the marginalized and the destitute. The correlate to crossing borders is a profound insertion into the streets where the disinherited and the needy walk everyday in order to plant a permanent parish tent in these critical places. The preliminary requirement is a conversion to the world of the marginalized that expresses itself in a radical transformation of lifestyle. The borders that must be crossed are many. But it is not exclusively about—as it has been traditionally understood in evangelical circles—a crossing of geographic borders. Jesus did not cross borders of that kind to encounter the

---

12. Ford, "Reconciliation and Forgiveness," 85.

tax collector Matthew.[13] Jesus crossed the cultural, social, and religious borders of his time. Likewise, following the example of Jesus, we must cross all of these borders or subcultures in which the marginalized, the excluded, and the banished of society are found. This task is never easy, especially since it demands an inversion of values and an unwavering commitment to the Lord of mission.

THE CALL TO FOLLOW

The tax collector Levi or Matthew did not take the initiative in following Jesus. It was Jesus who presented him with the invitation to follow him.[14] Luke and the other gospels indicate that no one summons him or her self to discipleship or designates him or her self as a disciple of Jesus. In his gospel Mark emphatically remarks that Jesus "called to him those whom he wanted" (Mark 3:13). So it is indeed. The calling of Matthew the publican, recorded in the synoptic gospels, confirms this principle (Matt 9:9; Mark 2:14; Luke 5:27). Jesus deliberately chose this tax collector, excluded and spurned by the Jews, to be his disciple. The words of Jesus when he invited him to follow him, *akolouthei moi* or follow me, indicate that it was not a casual, optional, or deferrable matter. It was an order that left no room for delays, excuses, or pretences. According to Darrell Bock, the almost instantaneous response of Matthew the publican reveals both the reputation that Jesus had at the moment and the quality of an exemplary response to the invitation made by him.[15] The Lucan account is very clear in this regard when it emphasizes that Matthew placed following Jesus as the immediate priority of his life (Luke 5:28).

Why did Matthew the publican respond in this way to the invitation made by Jesus? What can be derived from the Lucan account, especially when taking into account the position of publicans in the Jewish society of the time, is that for this despised and rejected tax collector, being a disciple of Christ meant coming out of the social ostracism he was in due

13. We also must cross geographical borders. But that is not the only kind of border that Jesus' disciples had to cross in order to carry out their missionary call. In our own mission contexts there is a series of cultural and social borders that must be crossed, for example, the border of street children or the border of the world of politics.

14. This is a distinctive mark of discipleship that the synoptic gospels unanimously record (Matt 4:19, 21; 8:22; 9:9; Mark 1:17, 20; 2:14; 3:13; Luke 5:27; 6:13). The same idea is also present in the gospel of John (1:35–51).

15. Bock, *Luke*, 107–8.

to his occupation and his conduct. In other words, the fact that Jesus invited him to become part of the community of disciples implies the social redemption of this man who went from being a social outcast to being considered as a human being created in the image of God, from marginalization to comradeship. The call to discipleship thus has a concrete social and political effect, as those marginalized by the system find in the community of disciples an alternative community that dignifies them as human beings. This alone calls into question the pyramid of power of the predominant society and all forms of marginalization and exclusion that assault human dignity.

Discipleship is always a challenge to follow Jesus and not merely the acceptance of a set of religious regulations, a moral code, a theological perspective, or an ecclesiastical identity. Nor is it incorporation into a determined religious community, loyalty to a particular doctrine, or identification with a charismatic spiritual leader. According to the gospels, discipleship is always a following of Christ. It is a following that comes with a precise cost, which expresses itself in the challenge to feel, think, and act as disciples within a society governed by values different from the values of the kingdom of God. In the words of Bonhoeffer:

> When we are called to follow Christ, we are summoned to an exclusive attachment to his person. The grace of his call bursts all the bonds of legalism. It is a gracious call, a gracious commandment. It transcends the difference between the law and the gospel. Christ calls, the disciple follows: that is grace and commandment in one. . . . Discipleship means adherence to Christ, and, because Christ is the object of that adherence, it must take the form of discipleship.[16]

Accordingly, it is not about staying faithful to a determined religion, nor a simple adoption of certain liturgical practices, or about having firm ethical principles. It is about having a close relationship with the person of Jesus, an unbreakable connection to him, a total identification with him who called us. The correlate of this relationship and this identification with Jesus of Nazareth is feeling, thinking, and acting, having as an unshakable foundation the principles of the kingdom of God and his justice.

---

16. Bonhoeffer, *Cost of Discipleship*, 63.

THE COST OF DISCIPLESHIP

The gospels of Matthew and Mark, when they tell of the calling of Levi or Matthew, simply note that this tax collector "got up and followed him" (Matt 9:9; Mark 2:14). Only Luke specifies that Matthew the publican "got up, left everything, and followed him" (Luke 5:28). What is unique to the Lucan account is the expression "left everything." Why does Luke underline this fact? In Luke 9:57–62, an exclusively Lucan text that explains the conditions of radical discipleship, the same idea is expressed. That is, the path of discipleship has as a preliminary condition leaving everything behind for the cause of Jesus. Matthew the publican understood that demand when Jesus called him to follow him. He realized that following Jesus entailed complete renunciation of all exaggerated attachment to material goods. This fact really stands out when one keeps in mind that tax collectors were usually extremely prosperous in economic terms, and, for that reason, Matthew had to make a lofty sacrifice when he renounced his occupation as a publican,[17] especially since the lucrative occupation of publican—the fortune of an employee of the Roman Empire—guaranteed him secure economic benefits, certain economic stability, and a future free of financial uncertainties. For a tax collector like Matthew, accustomed to a life where fraud, extortion, and deceit were considered normal, it certainly was not easy to abandon this dishonest way of making money. But Jesus invited him to reorient his priorities, to change his way of life, to run the risk of being vulnerable for his sake, and to place all of his trust in him and not in his material possessions.

The experience of Matthew the publican shows that discipleship has a necessary cost that is expressed in the capacity to renounce exaggerated attachment to worldly things that have turned into idols that we serve. Following Jesus demands renouncing the life cycle that provides us with security and gives us a name, certain prestige, and worldly power. Jurgen Moltmann, commenting on the calling of Abraham, expresses the following in regards to this close relationship between calling and renunciation:

> Evidently [Abraham] trusted in the word of promise more than in all the securities of his life "beyond the River." He left the familiar patterns of his life which had provided a home and security for him. He abandoned his fatherland and became an alien. He left his friends and was alone. He left his father's house and

17. Morris, *Gospel According to Matthew*, 219–20.

lost his identity. He even left his gods . . . and became a god-less person who alone followed the call of the unknown "Lord." The Bible calls this "faith": leaving the dwelling places of reality where one has peace and security and giving oneself over to the course of history, to the way of freedom and danger, the way of disappointment and surprise, borne along and led solely by God's hope.[18]

In following Jesus, the calling cannot be separated from the cost and the renunciation that this radical commitment implies. We err when we lower the cost of discipleship in order to obtain better numerical results that secure our place in the ecclesiastic hierarchy or that are useful to us to maintain the prestige obtained in certain religious circles, and when we convert the gospel into another article on the contemporary religious market as if it were a simple product sold in a modern supermarket or a piece of chicken offered at Kentucky Fried Chicken. In order to be pertinent, in order that our discourse may be "believable" and relevant, we do not need to renounce our Christian identity and present the gospel as a cheap ideology adaptable for mass consumption. Discipleship has a cost; it demands real renunciations; it calls for a radical reorientation of values. This cost, requirement, and demand cannot be and should never be lowered. This is how Matthew the publican understood it. We must understand it in the same way.

SOLIDARITY WITH THE MARGINALIZED

In the accounts of Matthew and Mark, it is not clear who organized the banquet, Jesus or Levi (Matt 9:10; Mark 2:15), but in Luke it is explicitly mentioned that it was the tax collector who threw the banquet: "Then Levi gave a great banquet for him in his house" (Luke 5:29). When Matthew organized this banquet in his house, a party that he invited the other publicans and marginalized like himself to, Jesus accepted the invitation to enter into the house of this known public sinner and to participate in a party where individuals scorned and hated by the Jews were present.[19] According to the Jewish religious standards of the time, this was a scandal

---

18. Moltmann, *Experiment Hope*, 47–48.

19. Luke's gospel also contains another account of Jesus entering into the house of a known public sinner, Zacchaeus, a chief tax collector (Luke 19:5–7).

which placed "him and his disciples in a condition of ritual impurity."[20] Jesus' attitude, which called into question the social practices considered by the Jews to be proper and normal, like the exclusion and contempt they had for publicans, explains why the scribes and the Pharisees began to complain and formulated a question that clearly expressed their theological point of view and religious prejudices: "Why do you eat and drink with tax collectors and sinners?" (Luke 5:30). The question put forth here is, why would Jesus participate in this banquet, sitting at the same table as many publicans? What was his intention? In light of the Lucan view of the liberating mission of Jesus, an act such as Jesus' presence in the house of a known public sinner in the company of many marginalized has a particular theological significance.[21] It is a clear indicator both of the inclusivity of God's love and of his special love for the marginalized, the social scum, and the outcasts. On this subject, R.T. France notes that sharing a meal with others constituted a sign of intimacy, therefore, Jesus' presence in the house of Matthew the publican expressed his willingness "to identify himself with the undesirable."[22] Taking into account this key fact pertaining to the cultural world of the first century, Jesus' intention is sufficiently clear, as he himself expressed when faced with the social critique of the scribes and Pharisees: "Those who are well have no need of a physician, but those who are sick; I have come to call not the righteous but sinners to repentance" (Luke 5:31–32). Or as Joachim Jeremias has stated:

> Jesus' table community entails something more: the proclamation of the time of salvation has already burst forth. . . . The surprising thing is that sinners and publicans are counted among the companions at the table of the family of God. Peoples of the Near East, for whom symbolic action had a much greater significance than it does for us, immediately understood that the admission of religiously and morally excluded persons to the table community of Jesus signified the offering of salvation to sinners and the granting of forgiveness. . . . Only by beginning with this understanding can one grasp the limitless gratitude of Zacchaeus when Jesus entered into his house, the house of a hated chief tax collector (Luke 19:1–10), and only in this way can one understand the passionate protest of the Pharisees, which in effect was an invitation to the disciples to separate themselves

20. Ford, *My Enemy Is My Guest*, 71; see also Gnilka, *Evangelio Según San Marcos*, 124.

21. Ford, *My Enemy Is My Guest*, 71.

22. France, *Matthew*, 167.

from a man who maintained relations with impure friends (Mark 2:16; Luke 15:2; cf. Luke 19:7). Jesus' message, which proclaims the God who desires to relate with sinners, found in the table community with the scorned its clearest expression, but also its most shocking.[23]

The disciples of Jesus, following his example, must be open to sitting at the same table as publicans and sinners of this time. This identification, which should express itself in solidarity practice, is more than a term used to justify particular political options or certain social service projects with selfish interests; it must be a channel for expressing our commitment to life. When we sit at the table with other human beings who do not share our worldview and do not think like us, we are not negotiating the singularity of Christ, and we are not denying our evangelical identity or endorsing some form of syncretism. On the contrary, we recognize and value the image of God in others, we confess our humanity, we become vulnerable and accessible to others, and we learn that dialogue is more valuable than monologue. We all need to learn to share the communion bread at the table of the disinherited, under the roof of those forgotten and marginalized by "official history," smelling the aroma of their dreams kept down by years of structural violence. God walks on this road. He sees what we sometimes are incapable of seeing due to our theological prejudices and our ideological presuppositions. God always has a moment to sit at the table of those who "decent folk" classify as non-persons. God does not fear breathing the air that the marginalized breathe every day.

We all must understand that our Christian commitment and the theological foundation that sustains it become "believable" when this coherence exists between religious discourse and the lifestyle of the people who incarnate it. In this sense, human needs are much more important than each day's agenda, than the priorities of institutions, than work schedules and monthly reports. The value of a person is superior to cultural and social prejudices, greater than political or religious interests, and before the operating plans of institutions. It will never be a loss of time to sit at the table with the marginalized. The key phrase is a change of values, therefore, a transformation of the aim of life. Following Jesus

---

23. Jeremias, *Mensaje Central*, 262, my translation. While an English version of this book exists (*Central Message of the New Testament*), the chapter quoted from ("Esto Es Mi Cuerpo" [This Is My Body]) is not included in the English edition.

demands a commitment to the Life. And it is almost certain that on this path of renunciations and daily risks, just as in the past, the contemporary scribes and Pharisees will grumble and ask: "Why do you eat and drink with tax collectors and sinners?" (Luke 5:30). But this is the risk and also the challenge for disciples today.

4

And He Gave Him to His Mother

When the Fragile Encounter the God of Life

Luke 7:11–17

INTRODUCTION

Jesus valued and dealt in a special way with fragile social sectors and the unprotected, like women. The way that he valued and treated them stands out even more if one keeps in mind that in the cultural world of first century Palestine, women made up part of the world of the excluded and the less privileged.[1] In a society that considered them as insignificant and as less important than men, Jesus saw them and valued them as human beings created in the image of God and as beneficiaries of the kingdom of God that he proclaimed.[2] The third gospel testifies to the particular concern or special interest that he had for the defenseless and

---

1. Bock, *Luke*, 200; Marshall, "Luke," 887.
2. Senior and Stuhlmueller, *Biblical Foundations for Mission*, 260–61.

underprivileged social sectors like women (Luke 7:11–17, 36–50; 8:2–3, 40–56; 10:38–42; 13:10–17; 21:1–4; 23:27–28, 49, 55; 24:1–12). This New Testament document frequently remarks that Jesus of Nazareth, when he began to proclaim the good news of the kingdom of God from the spurned province of Galilee, was neither insensitive nor indifferent to the various human needs of the marginalized. The Teacher from Galilee always had time to see, to listen to, to pay attention to, and to help the marginalized whom he had dealings with and related with daily.

So, one day in the town of Nain, he had compassion on a widow who was crying over the death of her only son. In the account of this instance, which is recorded only in Luke's gospel, the concrete gestures of love that Jesus displayed toward this woman, who was grieving and without hope due to the death of the only one—her son—who could guarantee her a dignified life in the future, outline the missional route that the disciples of the carpenter from Nazareth must travel in all missional contexts. It is a route that is connected to the way they daily value, treat, and relate with vulnerable and unprotected social sectors like grieving and abandoned mothers.

THE REAL PROBLEM

The pastoral challenges that Christian communities of distinct historical backgrounds and theological perspectives have to face each day in their respective missionary contexts are many and have diverse characteristics. There are not set prescriptions or response menus for confronting each of these challenges. In each situation, both the form of approaching the social problems and the actions that must be taken to resolve them may be completely different. Regarding this, the gospels testify that the way Jesus of Nazareth examined and resolved the problems affecting the human beings of flesh and bone, with whom he dealt and related during his missionary journeys, did not necessarily follow the same route to resolution each time. An examination of the Lucan accounts pertaining to the liberating mission of Jesus reveals this.

This is the case, for example, of the account of the resurrection of the only son of the widow from Nain.[3] In his gospel Luke describes the encounter that Jesus had with this widow during his missionary travels

---

3. Luke's gospel also records another case of a resurrection that took place during Jesus' traveling ministry. It is the account of the resurrection of the only daughter of Jairus (Luke 8:40–42, 49–56).

through the region of Galilee (Luke 7:11). The scene that Luke describes took place in the town of Nain, which was likely located about 6 miles southeast of Nazareth.[4] A widow—it is not specified how long she had been one—had lost her only son (Luke 7:12). In first century Jewish culture, being a woman and a widow meant having an enormous disadvantage as opposed to other persons who had the protection and care of a family circle. Moreover, one should not forget that, according to the cultural patterns of the first century, women were considered as less important than men and were situated in the lowest stratum of society, together with publicans, lepers, and Samaritans. Even more, this widow, whose age we do not know, had been left totally abandoned with the death of her only son. Her problem was truly tragic. With the death of her only son, on one hand, she had lost the hope of perpetuating the family line and having descendents.[5] On the other hand, she had been left alone in a hostile world with no one to protect her or watch over her material needs. The condition of material orphanhood that she was left in was extremely severe, especially since there were few opportunities for a woman to work to support herself in the first century.[6] Her future seemed dismal and uncertain.

The scene described by Luke in his gospel is incredibly dramatic. When Jesus arrived in the town of Nain, he saw a funeral procession and a poor woman crying in great distress over the loss of her only son. The fact that Luke underlines in his account the woman's social situation as a widow suggests that for him, the condition of material orphanhood that this woman was left in was extremely terrible. Due to the death of her only son—she had no other son—there was no guarantee of a dignified future for her. Rather, her survival in the coming years would be in the hands of pious folk, and she would depend on the charity of her neighbors for her daily sustenance. The situation of utter abandonment that she was left in due to the death of her only son was not pleasant in any way. Jesus, seeing her situation of orphanhood and knowing that she would have many material needs in the future, was concerned with the present and the immediate future of this widow. Jesus' actions of love were not limited to expressing a compassion disconnected from concrete gestures of solidarity. He gave clear demonstrations of love for and understanding of the widow's situation. The words that Jesus uttered in front of the

4. Hendriksen, *Luke*, 382; Morris, *Luke*, 153.

5. Hendriksen, *Luke*, 384.

6. Morris, *Luke*, 153.

crowd that accompanied the funeral procession—"Do not weep" (Luke 7:13)—were words of hope that subsequently translated into a miracle that returned to the widow the joy that she had lost with the death of her only son. In this way, Jesus presented himself as the Lord of life, whose liberating mission aimed to transform the living conditions of fragile human beings like this widow.

The lesson derived from the first part of this story is quite clear. Like Jesus of Nazareth, his disciples at that time who confessed him as Lord and Savior also had to concern themselves with the distinct concrete needs of human beings of flesh and bone. Indifference toward the manifold human needs of the fragile and unprotected and insensitivity toward the cry of our neighbor are not evangelical virtues, nor is insensitivity toward the pain and distress of the so many defenseless and destitute of the world. Active solidarity, whose point of departure is the capacity to see human needs and whose correlate is compassion, beyond being a clear gospel principle is also a visible expression of the presence of God among us. Jesus did not just see a funeral procession (Luke 7:12). He saw a widow, grieved and deserted, helpless and unprotected (Luke 7:12–13). He also saw beyond the present problem. He saw the immediate future of this woman. We must do the same. We must see the concrete problem of the fragile of today and tirelessly work to reverse their future. The distressed who are treated like social trash or human waste need to be consoled not only with palliatives that resolve urgent or day to day issues, but also with the establishment of better living conditions based in active solidarity aimed at the justice of the kingdom of God.

THE COMPASSION OF JESUS

The problem affecting the widow from Nain, from the human point of view, presented itself as unsolvable and irremediable. There was nothing to be done but bury the deceased. All human hope had ended with the boy's death. The widow, due to the cultural regulations of the time, was not left with any other recourse but to resign herself to the uncertain future that awaited her. She had to prepare herself to beg for her daily sustenance thereafter and depend on public charity. However, as Luke reports, Jesus was not indifferent to the situation of hopelessness in which this widow found herself (Luke 7:13–14). The first words that Jesus uttered before the multitude that accompanied the funeral procession were not rude gestures or gestures lacking in kindness or understanding of her real problem. Jesus' compassion, first expressed in the words, "Do not weep," intended to communicate a glimmer of hope to the grieved woman. According to Luke: "When the Lord saw her, he had compassion for her and said to her, 'Do not weep'" (Luke 7:13). After passing on this word of hope to the woman, Jesus' compassion went much further still. The act of touching the plank and requesting that those carrying the deceased stop (Luke 7:13) shows Jesus' intention of going beyond mere words and sporadic gestures of compassion.[7] In reality it was already a highly significant gesture for a rabbi like Jesus, an expert on the religious regulations of his time, to touch the plank with the dead person on it, as he ran the risk of being declared ceremonially unclean due to his physical contact with a dead person.[8] Why did he do it? No doubt the key to comprehending this attitude of Jesus should be sought in the understanding that he had of the human person as a creation of God. For Jesus, much more important than the religious prejudices of his time or the predominant cultural patterns of his historical context, were the human beings in need of the grace of God.

Jesus' compassion did not limit itself, therefore, to the simple expression of words of consolation or to certain hesitant and sporadic actions of brotherly love. Jesus' compassion expressed itself in concrete actions of solidarity that aimed to resolve the problems affecting people. What Jesus did for the widow from Nain clearly expresses the solidary practice that he had, and it presents itself as a model that the disciples of that time, following Jesus' example, had to follow in all missional frontiers in which they might find themselves giving testimony—in word and deed—of the good news of the kingdom of God. The excluded and helpless, more than words of consolation that transmit hope in a social climate where desperation and distress are common, need these words to be translated into concrete material gestures that acknowledge the integral salvation that comes from the proclamation of the good news of the kingdom of God. In his gospel Luke underlines that Jesus of Nazareth is the hope of the fragile. When they encounter him, it totally changes their purpose in life, because Jesus reverses their destiny, transforming pain into joy and loneliness into comradeship.

7. According to Hendriksen, the stretcher was a portable, simple, and open device, upon which the corpse was placed. It perhaps was a "flat board equipped with staves and poles" (*Luke*, 390).

8. Bock, *Luke*, 135.

A MOTHER'S JOY

Jesus' presence in this woman's life, when she was passing through a critical situation, transformed her pain into joy. Jesus' gestures of love toward this widow from Nain were intended to show that he cared greatly about human beings and their concrete needs. The Lord Jesus is not indifferent to the reality of grief and desperation in which many people find themselves. Just as he took note of and resolved the problem of the widow from Nain, returning to her the son she had lost, so also today he shows his affection for and solidarity with all those who come to him seeking help.

In his gospel Luke records the miracle performed by Jesus on that occasion in this way: "And he said, 'Young man, I say to you, rise!' The dead man sat up and began to speak" (Luke 7:14–15). The fact that Jesus spoke to a dead person, according to Luke's account, is rather curious and seems like nonsense. Even more, according to common sense and to scientific opinion, it may seem out of place for miracles like that described by Luke in his gospel to occur. But Luke presents the events, not as simple incidents or as a story for misled children, but as events that really took place. The authentic proof of the resurrection of the widow's only son was in the fact that once he got up from the bier he was in, he began to articulate words as an undoubted sign that he had come back to life (Luke 7:15). Another fact, not always taken into account in the analysis of these events, is the way that Luke describes the relationship that Jesus established with the widow. Luke mentions that, following the resurrection of the widow's son, Jesus "gave him to his mother" (Luke 7:15). In other words, the woman, whose immense grief was understandable, was a privileged eye-witness of the love of God in action. Even more, she could see how Jesus not only brought the son she had lost back to life, but herself as well. As the resurrection of her only son, in light of the situation of utter material orphanhood in which she had been left, meant her own social resurrection. This is especially the case because, with the resurrection of her only son, the widow recovered the only person who could guarantee her a dignified life and access to daily food in the future. This explains why, when faced with the miracle carried out by Jesus, the crowd that had been accompanying the funeral procession reacted in the following way: "Fear seized all of them; and they glorified God, saying, 'A great prophet has risen among us!' and 'God has looked favorably on his people!'" (Luke 7:16).

When Jesus observed the problem of the widow from Nain, he did what she least expected: he resurrected her only son.[9] Jesus always surprises us. He acts at the moment when we least expect it. When the fragile—like the widow in the Lucan account—encounter the God of life, who has a special love for all who are in a situation of disadvantage, are never the same following this encounter. The God of life changes both their present and their future. This is what occurred with the widow from Nain. A woman on her way to bury her only son, following her encounter with Jesus and in the midst of her pain and agony as a mother, returned to house with her heart full of joy, for her only son was alive again. The expression "God has visited His people" (Luke 7:16, NAS) suggests that for the witnesses of this event, the miracle performed by Jesus of Nazareth on this occasion constituted an unequivocal sign of God's love in action on the stage of history.[10] God was present in Jesus of Nazareth, and the fragile of the time could feel, within their own reality of exclusion and material misery, that he had come to reverse their destiny. And so it is indeed. When the fragile encounter the God of life, the joy produced by this encounter transforms all of the material conditions of their existence and transmits to them a love for the life that no earthly lord can snatch away from them. The fragile have him as their *goël*, their vindicator, the one who loses face for them, the one who defends them. The fragile like the widow from Nain are not alone. God is on their side. And the God of life has the power to defeat death and misery.

9. This miracle is reminiscent of the resurrections carried out in the time of the Old Testament by the prophets Elijah (1 Kgs 17:17–24) and Elisha (2 Kgs 4:32–37).

10. The visitation of God is one of the theological themes present in the Lucan work. See, for example, texts like Luke 1:68, 78; 19:41–44; Acts 15:14.

5

Go and Do Likewise

A Marginal as a Model of a Neighbor

Luke 10:25–37

INTRODUCTION

Jesus of Nazareth taught profound spiritual truths and authoritative moral lessons positioned to transform the narrow mentality of the religious folk of his time and the predominant social relations of exclusion in the cultural climate of the first century, not by means of complex theological discourse or intricate theoretical musings aimed at satisfying the intellectual curiosity of the learned, but through stories taken from real life situations that were familiar to those listening. The parables of Jesus were more than simple literary recourses to capture the attention of a certain audience or conversational bridges to relate with determined persons; they had a clear pedagogical intention supported by a firm theological foundation. Regarding this, Joachim Jeremias points out that the parables "reflect with peculiar clarity the character of his good news, the eschatological nature of his preaching, [and] the intensity of his summons to repentance."[1] And David Wenham asserts that when Jesus spoke to the multitudes that followed him, he did so pedagogically, explaining his teachings through stories.[2] As Wenham states, "[Jesus] used parables not simply to add spice to his teaching, but in order also to involve people personally in his ministry and to challenge people very directly with his message."[3]

The parable of the Good Samaritan—an exclusively Lucan parable (Luke 10:25–37)—is an excellent example of the way that the teacher from Galilee confronted his listeners with the good news of the kingdom of God. This parable outlines practical principles, with a clear pedagogical intention, pertaining to the universal nature of mission and to God's special love for the marginalized and the ragged of society.[4] It teaches that one's neighbor—and who we should be and act as a neighbor to—is not determined by race, religious creed, social status, culture, or gender, but by the fact that others—those who have fallen down on the road—are human beings created in the image of God.[5] The story told by Jesus presents a practical example of love in action, free of preference and partiality.[6] It stresses that love, forgiveness, and acceptance of the enemy are clear marks that characterize the new covenant community.

In order to capture its theological vigor and its ethical scope, one must take into account certain historical, geographical, and social facts pertaining to the temporal context in which Jesus told this parable, as this information allows one to analyze the biblical text in its concrete historical context. The first piece of information one should consider is the religious, cultural, and social situation of the Samaritans. In the cultural world of the first century, Jews treated the Samaritans as semi-pagans, semi-foreigners, bad neighbors, and a mixed race with whom they sought to have the least physical contact possible. They avoided all forms of so-

---

1. Jeremias, *Parables of Jesus*, 11.

2. Wenham, *Parables of Jesus*, 12–13.

3. Wenham, "Last Supper," 11.

4 With the pericope of the Good Samaritan, Luke introduces the theology of mission to the Gentiles, a theme later developed in Acts 8, and that should have seemed completely unacceptable to the majority of the extremely nationalist and revolutionary Jewish sectors of the time (Ford, *My Enemy Is My Guest*, 92).

5. Bock, *Luke*, 199.

6. Craddock, *Luke*, 151.

cial relations with them.[7] Some very religious Jews considered them as inhuman. Even more, from some Jewish perspectives, "the Samaritans were enemies not only of the Jews, but also of God."[8] As descendents of a mixed population that occupied this geographic region following the conquest by the Assyrians in 722 BCE, the Samaritans were considered as ceremonially unclean, socially marginal, and religiously heretical.[9] The words of a woman belonging to this mixed race, during the dialogue that Jesus had with her in the Samaritan city of Sychar (John 4:5–26), express part of the problem of social and religious relations that existed between them and the Jews. These were her words: "'How is it that you, a Jew, ask a drink of me, a woman of Samaria?' (Jews do not share things in common with Samaritans)" (John 4:9). According to Joachim Jeremias: "The relations between the Jews and the mixed peoples, which had undergone considerable fluctuations, had become very much worse in the time of Jesus, after the Samaritans, between AD 6 and 9 at midnight, during a Passover, had defiled the temple court by strewing a dead man's bones; as a result irreconcilable hostility existed between the two parties."[10]

It is noteworthy that, knowing the background of the historical enmity between Jews and Samaritans, according to the Lucan testimony, Jesus healed a Samaritan suffering from leprosy (Luke 17:11–19) and used one of them as an example of a neighbor (Luke 10:30–37). From the Lucan view, Jesus had a special love for the marginal sectors like the Samaritans, a people who also needed to hear the good news of salvation and enjoy the benefits of the kingdom. Or, as Wenham states, Luke emphasizes that the kingdom of God is principally good news for the poor, for the marginalized, and for the excluded.[11]

The second important thing to consider is the conditions of the road between Jerusalem and Jericho.[12] The Jews were familiar with the high risk involved in traveling alone along a relatively long route—approximately

---

7. Bock, *Luke*, 197; Wenham, *Parables of Jesus*, 156; Wenham, "Last Supper," 12.

8. Bosch, *Transforming Mission*, 90.

9. Craddock, *Luke*, 150.

10. Jeremias, *Parables of Jesus*, 204.

11. Wenham, *Parables of Jesus*, 154.

12. John A. Mackay says that: "These two cities were about twenty miles apart. Setting out from Jerusalem from the plateau, the road that connects them winds downhill through the mountains until arriving at the Jordan Valley, where Jericho is located, over three thousand feet below the elevation of the capital" ("*Mas Yo Os Digo,*" 178, my translation).

seventeen miles—known for being a place where assaults on travelers were quite frequent. This explains why people traveled in groups or in caravans.[13] Regarding this, John A. Mackay holds that: "From the remotest of times this pass has enjoyed a bad reputation and it earned the name of 'Bloody Road' due to the large number of assaults and murders that continuously occurred there."[14] These particular facts pertaining to the conditions and potential dangers of the road between Jerusalem and Jericho allow us to understand why, according to Luke, "A man who was going down from Jerusalem to Jericho, and fell into the hands of robbers, who stripped him, beat him, and went away, leaving him half dead" (Luke 10:30).

THE CONTEXT OF THE PARABLE

The story told by Jesus is preceded by the questions of an interpreter of the law. This learned theologian, according to Luke's testimony, asked the following question to test Jesus: "Teacher . . . what must I do to inherit eternal life?" (Luke 10:25). Jesus, instead of responding directly to the question of the specialist in religious topics, asked him two more questions, thus forcing the interpreter of the law to reflect on them: "What is written in the law? What do you read there?" (Luke 10:26). The immediate reply of this Jewish academic (Luke 10:27) reveals that deep down he knew the answer to his own question. This indicates that the problem was not at the theoretical level, but in the practical consequences of Deut 6:5 and Lev 19:18, two Old Testament passages upon which this expert on the Pentateuch based his response, addressing the questions posed by Jesus. From a theological point of view, the interpreter of the law's answer was correct—"You have given the right answer," was what Jesus commented on the religious man's response (Luke 10:28)—but his religious prejudices were stronger than the commandment to love his neighbor. For this reason, he formulated a new question: "And who is my neighbor?" (Luke 10:29). In order to understand the intention that was behind this new question posed by this clever Jewish theologian, articulated "to justify himself" (Luke 10:29), one must understand the concept of neighbor that the pious Jews had at the time. According to René Padilla: "The distinction between 'neighbor' and 'foreigner' made it possible for the Jew to understand Leviticus 19:18 as a call to a love that limited itself to the

13. Wenham, "Last Supper," 11.
14. Mackay, *"Mas Yo Os Digo"*, 179, my translation.

conational and excluded the Gentile. So, then, the question of the rabbi ('And who is my neighbor?') reflects a traditional interpretation of the commandment of God that the teacher of the law takes refuge in before Jesus Christ."[15]

Or as John A. Mackay specifies:

> For every pious Jew the term "neighbor" was equivalent to "conational." The inhabitants of the holy nation did not recognize their obligation to love their geographical neighbors on the other side of the border. And yet even within this native land there existed the increasingly marked tendency to establish categories of proximity among members of the same race.[16]

It is thus clear that for this interpreter of the law, this academic accustomed to intellectual exercise, his preoccupation was with concepts and theoretical definitions. Jesus did not fall into his game; on the contrary, with his questions he compelled this clever theologian to relate his knowledge to practical life. He forced him to put aside his religious and cultural prejudices in order to expand his theological horizon concerning his neighbor.

The theological "excuse" ("And who is my neighbor?") of the interpreter of the law recurs when evangelicals today discuss if the duty of loving one's neighbor forms part of the missionary vocation of the church or not, when they teach that the defense of human life is a task outside of the Christian commitment, or when they marginalize other persons, placing their religious prejudices and political interests above the commandment to love their neighbor. Who is my neighbor? The answer to this question seems quite clear for evangelicals; it has highly prophetic content, above all in this time in which our consumer society considers millions of human beings as simple instruments of the invisible hand of the market or as disposable pieces subject to the law of supply and demand. The parable of the Good Samaritan affirms active solidarity in contrast to selfish individualism and proposes an unyielding commitment to the defense of human dignity in contrast to religious superficiality insensitive to human needs.

15. Padilla, "Ser Prójimo," 148, my translation.
16. Mackay, "Mas Yo Os Digo," 177, my translation.

THE PROBLEM

Jesus starts the parable by describing the concrete problem. The picture is incredibly dramatic. He describes the critical situation in which the human being who fell into the hands of thieves found himself, was stripped of his possessions, and was half-dead on the road that descended from Jerusalem to Jericho (Luke 10:30). There is no information about the life history of the assault victim. The only fact mentioned in the parable is that he was a man (*ánthropos*). In the words of Padilla:

> If anything calls my attention in this parable, it is that no information regarding the victim attacked by the thieves is given; the only fact given is that he was a man, nothing more. His age, his profession, his race, his ideology, the intentions of his trip, if he was rich or poor, we do not know. The only thing we know is that he was a human being, a man who fell into the hands of thieves, and that is enough.[17]

The need of this man lying half-dead on the road was apparently enough. The priority was not to take inventory of his primary pressing needs or to analyze the factors that generated this situation. Nor was it to calculate the advantages and disadvantages of stopping to help him, or wonder if it was first necessary to theologize regarding this problem, and afterward, newly think about what could be done to cure his wounds. What a neighbor had to do in this moment was clear enough and did not require a greater explanation.

Two religious men of Jewish nationality, a priest and a Levite, saw the problem and passed by on the other side of the road (Luke 10:31–32). In the parable no reason is given to explain the conduct of these two persons, who at the very least one could expect, as religious men, to have compassion on this man who was half-dead on the road. To explain the indifference, both of the priest and of the Levite, Padilla has suggested some possible reasons:

> It is most probable that if we had them before us, they would know how to explain their attitude. They could mention, for example, a practical reason: they were in a hurry. Or a prudent reason: it was advisable to move him from that place, but under pain of being assaulted themselves or (who knows?) accused of the attack. Or, even better, a religious reason, with a biblical

17. Padilla, "Opción Galilea," 22, my translation.

foundation: if the man was half-dead, touching him meant con-
taminating oneself, as according to the Old Testament, "He who
touches the corpse of any person will be unclean for seven days"
(Numbers 9:11). In short, to assist the fallen it would have been
necessary to face a risk, and, who wants to take a risk to help
someone they do not know?[18]

These and other excuses or pretexts may explain the apathy and indifference of the religious of yesterday and of today, when faced with concrete needs of human beings. As Padilla says, based on the argument of
this parable, the priest and the Levite were "religious but inhuman folk."[19]
The lack of sensitivity and the indifference of the priest and of the Levite
reveal that in reality they did not see the problem, as Cook suggests:
"Seeing without acting is in reality not seeing."[20] Like certain religious
contemporaries, evangelical and non-evangelical, those in charge of the
worship service and of the sacrifices in the Jerusalem temple (priests)
and their assistants (Levites), either because they were in a hurry or due
to their theological prejudices or their fear of danger, they did not have
time to attend to the "things of this world" or to "worldly matters." Both
opted to evade the problem. The lesson is quite clear. Religious prejudices and fear of the consequences that come from the act of seeing the
pressing needs of human beings of flesh and bone immersed in concrete
conditions of oppression and marginalization can condition or limit one's
vision of reality and paralyze actions of love toward one's neighbor.

THE DILEMMA

A Samaritan enters onto the scene. It must have been a tremendous surprise to the Jews that in place of mentioning them, as they certainly expected, as the third character in the Jewish trilogy (a priest, a Levite, and
a lay Israelite), Jesus placed a marginal and scorned Samaritan as a model
of a neighbor. In the words of Jeremias: "It would have been completely
unexpected and disconcerting for them to hear that the third character,
who fulfilled the duty of love, was a Samaritan."[21] The Samaritan, according to the parable, passed through the same road where moments before

18. Padilla, "Ser Prójimo," 149, my translation.
19. Ibid., my translation.
20. Cook, "Ver, Juzgar, y Actuar," 96, my translation.
21. Jeremias, *Parables of Jesus*, 204.

the priest and the Levite had travelled. But, in contrast to the first two, faced with the dilemma of passing by or remaining to help the person who had been assaulted, he chose the latter (Luke 10:33–35). The parable emphasizes that an individual who one would least expect to act as a neighbor, someone who was ungodly and inhuman according to the Jews, became a neighbor to the person who had fallen on the road. According to this story, the hero of the parable was an individual who was culturally considered as the last person who one would expect to act as an exemplary neighbor.[22] What singular act marked the difference between the two religious Jews and the Samaritan of the parable? What was unique to the Samaritan was not simply that he saw a man lying on the road (Luke 10:33), but that when he saw him, he was moved to mercy and "his heart went out to him."[23] And, consequently, he acted, propelled by love (Luke 10:34). The Lucan account states that: "But a Samaritan while traveling came near him; and when he saw him, he was moved with pity. He went to him and bandaged his wounds, having poured oil and wine on them. Then he put him on his own animal, brought him to an inn, and took care of him" (Luke 10:33–34).

The Samaritan did not side-step the responsibility of becoming a neighbor to a stranger. He did not pass by. He put aside the dilemma between passing by or staying. He chose to submerge himself in the problem of the other. He decided to help, spending his time and his resources, a human being fallen on the road. The parable emphasizes both the extreme generosity and the immense kindness of the Samaritan. He not only healed the wounds of the person lying on the road, but he also took him to a safe place and concerned himself with taking care of every last detail.[24] His compassion expressed itself in practical actions.

Undoubtedly, the actions of the Samaritan of the parable demand a radical change in values, a lifestyle transformation that expresses itself in concrete actions and a commitment to the defense of human dignity. It demands putting prejudices aside. As Padilla indicates: "The Samaritan was not bound by traditions, nor did he have hesitations that impeded him from acting according to the dictates of his heart, as in the case of the

22. Bock, *Luke*, 197.

23. Hendriksen, *Luke*, 594.

24. Leon Morris suggests that: "The Samaritan was paying about two months board. . . . J. Jeremias brings forward evidence that a day's rations cost a twelfth of a denarius at this time" (*Luke*, 208).

religious men. There was nothing to break the chain of self-giving love: seeing, having compassion, acting."[25]

What is the lesson for today? It is quite simple. Passing by when faced with human needs, when faced with the emergencies of persons who are half-dead on the road, is nothing other than a negation of the commandment to love our neighbor. In this sense, we must be alert when faced with the temptation to convert evangelical faith into a religion that justifies economic policies that treat human beings as if they are disposable things, and we must be first in line for an inescapable task such as defending the dignity of human beings as creations of God. The God of life has called us to see what others, due to their religious prejudices and wretched political interests, do not wish or desire to see. Compassion that leads to solidarity must be one of the distinct characteristics of evangelical identity, especially in this time where ambiguity and aversion to commitment, two visible marks of the contemporary global world, are infecting the Christian testimony with the virus of social demobilization and the virus of collective memory loss.

THE QUESTION

Jesus' question must have made the Jewish theologian incredibly uncomfortable: "Which of these three, do you think, was a neighbor to the man who fell into the hands of the robbers?" (Luke 10:36). This discomfort can be noted in his response to Jesus' question, as he avoids any direct reference to the Samaritan, thus trying not to utter the word that was so offensive to him: "The one who showed him mercy" (Luke 10:37). Regarding Jesus' question that sought to bring the intellectual from personal theoretical concerns and preoccupations to the practical level, Joachim Jeremias has noted the following: "Thus both Jesus and the scribe are after the same thing: they are not seeking a definition, but the extent of the conception *rea'* [comrade]: the only difference between them is that the scribe is looking at the matter from a theoretical point of view, while Jesus illuminates the question with a practical example."

The theological dilemma that the interpreter of the law had to resolve involved accepting that a Samaritan had acted as a neighbor and that, according to the parable, was presented as a model to follow. For a Jewish theologian, familiar with the law and with theoretical formulations,

25. Padilla, "Ser Prójimo," 149.

there must have been a very serious problem in having to recognize that only the semi-pagan and hated Samaritan had acted as a neighbor. With his question, Jesus sought for this specialist in Jewish law to expand his theological horizons by admitting that there were no limits for the meaning of neighbor. According to Joachim Jeremías: "In this parable Jesus tells his questioner that while the 'friend' is certainly, in the first place, his fellow-countryman, yet the meaning of the term is not limited to that. The example of the despised half-breed was intended to teach him that no human being was beyond the range of his charity. The law of love called him to be ready at any time to give his life for another's need."[26]

Expanding one's theological horizons is never an easy task. Admitting that love includes all people—even enemies—is always a task that demands renouncing prejudices of every kind. Seeing beyond particular religious borders is an endeavor that requires a transformation of values that inform and mold individual and collective conduct. Being and acting as a neighbor is a daily challenge, an invitation to commitment, a path to affirm the value of human life. In this sense, the question is not: who is my neighbor? The question is: am I behaving like a neighbor?

THE CHALLENGE

The final words of Jesus are very eloquent and commitment-invoking: "Go and do likewise" (Luke 10:37). For an interpreter of Jewish law, it must have been incredibly shocking to hear a "layman" like Jesus tell him to do the same as the Samaritan in the parable. In other words, that he must leave aside his religious and cultural prejudices in order to be and act as a neighbor. The challenge remains the same. Like the Samaritan in the parable, before calculating the costs and thinking of the risks, one must pay attention to and help those who are half-dead on the road. This is so, because watching over human needs does not require having vast resources or a large budget. The essential condition is learning to see reality, because only when we open our eyes do we discover human beings of flesh and bone. This form of seeing, based in compassion, always leads to commitment.

In our time, when prevailing theological fashions question the legitimacy of the social and political commitment of believers as part of their integral missionary responsibility, when the fight for human rights

---

26. Jeremias, *Parables of Jesus*, 205.

is criticized as being an improper and illegitimate task for evangelicals, and when it is thought that concern with worldly things devalues the transforming power of the gospel, Jesus' words to the interpreter of the law sound quite current, because doing the same as the Samaritan is the way of life that God expects of us. Theological understanding for its own sake, although it is a great asset, does not serve for much of anything when compassion, mercy, and solidarity are pushed aside. Faith in God demands expanding one's horizon of social relations and understanding that all human beings have been created in the image of God. This presupposes the rupture of prejudices that act as barriers separating people. One of the contemporary temptations is "passing by," avoiding all contact with historical reality. Seeing the drama of each day has, as a consequence, a call to commitment to change critical situations. Those who prefer not to commit themselves to the needs of others have "alternative" ways in their indifference and apathy. They so choose to follow the current of the present world in which ambiguity and disdain for commitment present themselves as paths that do not demand identifying oneself with a superior cause. John A. Mackay already observed this many years ago: "Sporadic charity is not sufficient, nor is systematic charity, for the alleviation of suffering; it lies primarily with the good Samaritans of today to show their human compassion in a way that contributes to doing away with the preventable causes of suffering. Here is a charity that is much more difficult, more complicated and prosaic than direct assistance on behalf of those in need."[27]

The demand of this hour is to be like the Samaritan of the parable. "Go and do likewise" still continues to be the challenge for this time. Jesus hopes that we will move from indifference and apathy to a commitment founded in compassion. In the words of Beda Rigaux: "He who listens to Jesus and obeys him should perceive the fundamental problem of charity, from man to man, above all when this man suffers and needs help, without asking for thanks, without looking at the price."[28]

Seeing others' needs, opening our hearts, and spending time and resources to resolve their immediate problems, are actions of love that identify us as a neighbor of others. Above selfishness that closes the heart and obscures vision, we should prefer solidarity and comradeship, because love for our neighbor is more important than love of money or excessive

27. Mackay, "*Mas Yo Os Digo*," 190, my translation.

28. Rigaux, *Historia de Jesús*, 189, my translation.

attachment to worldly things. Prejudices of every kind are always obstacles to love. Remaining at the level of theoretical speculation like the interpreter of the law, passing by like the priest and the Levite, or staying to help the fallen like the Samaritan are the life options that are also present on the contemporary scene. For the disciples of Jesus of Nazareth, the concrete challenge of this hour is to be and to act like the Samaritan in the parable. This requires understanding that self-giving love is specified or expressed in the chain: *seeing, compassion, action*. The decision is ours.

6

Woman, You Are Set Free from Your Ailment

Worship as Celebration of Life

Luke 13:10–17

INTRODUCTION

The sabbath or day of rest was established for the benefit of humankind.[1] From Jesus' perspective, the purpose of this day of rest was the integral wellbeing of all human beings: "The sabbath was made for humankind, and not humankind for the sabbath" (Mark 2:27). For him, the practice of good and the realization of good deeds on this holy day did not contradict the will of God in any way: "How much more valuable is a human being than a sheep! So it is lawful to do good on the sabbath" (Matt 12:12). Moreover, according to the unanimous testimony of the synoptic

1. The synoptic gospels record several occasions where Jesus and the religious of his time had disputes regarding the purpose of the day of rest (Matt 12:1–8, 9–14; Mark 2:23–28; 3:1–6; Luke 6:1–5, 6–11).

gospels, Jesus presented himself as the Lord of the day of rest (Matt 12:8; Mark 2:28; Luke 6:5). As Darrell Bock holds: "Jesus' action shows that the sabbath, like any day, is an appropriate time to minister and meet needs. It is perfectly permissible to do good on the sabbath."[2]

The Pharisees, zealous guardians of human tradition, had turned the day of rest into a time in which one had to fulfill a set of religious regulations that put limits on compassion. They had calculated that the law contained "248 commandments and 365 prohibitions"[3] and they boasted of strictly keeping these 613 religious arrangements. So, for example, they believed that it was forbidden to pluck the heads of grain on the sabbath (Luke 6:2), or to heal on this day in which, according to them, it was not permitted to liberate persons from their illnesses (Luke 6:7; 13:14). For these religious folk, the rules of their tradition and human commandments had more weight than the will of God and were placed above love for neighbor (Matt 12:9–14, Mark 3:1–6). They had forgotten that the essence of the law lies in the practice of justice, mercy, and faith (Matt 23:23). The Pharisees, through so many miniscule and sometimes absurd religious regulations, were transforming the sabbath into a cruel tyranny and humankind into a slave of that tyranny, as if the purpose of God had really been to make humankind for the day of rest rather than the day of rest for humankind.[4]

The healing of a woman who had been suffering from an ailment that prevented her from walking normally for eighteen years, a miracle that occurred on a day of rest, made clear the different points of view that Jesus and the religious folk of the time had regarding the meaning and purpose of the sabbath (Luke 13:10–17).[5] For the religious, when Jesus healed this woman, he was breaking the prohibition against working on this day. For Jesus, the liberation of this woman signified a fulfillment of the will of God that extended his love to all human beings. Jesus' compassionate gesture aimed to show that doing good on the day of rest was not contrary to God's commandment. Luke 13:10–17 is a paradigmatic biblical text that outlines several theological principles pertaining to the true worship of God. Jesus' actions in the synagogue on the day of rest

---

2. Bock, *Luke*, 117.

3. Stott, *Sermon on the Mount*, 74.

4. Hendriksen, *Mark*, 115.

5. In his gospel Luke also records other cases of healing or of liberation performed by Jesus on a day of rest (Luke 4:31–37; 6:6–11; 14:1–6).

indicate that compassion and mercy are not practices foreign to a genuine religious commitment, but on the contrary, they express that liberation from all types of oppression forms part of God's purpose. The healing of this ill woman, oppressed by Satan for eighteen years, affirms that the day of rest is a time to celebrate life.

In this paradigmatic biblical text, the Lucan concept of salvation is also present. This integral understanding of salvation does not separate onto irreconcilable planes the spiritual from the material, the sacred from the profane, or the individual from the communal. The words of Jesus, "Woman, you are set free from your ailment" (Luke 13:12), give account of this. In light of the Lucan testimony, the liberation proclaimed by Jesus on this occasion and on other occasions in which he encountered marginalized individuals and social outcasts (Luke 7:48, 50; 8:48, 17:19; 18:42), was an integral liberation.

THE INITIATIVE IN MISSION

For the regular synagogue attendees—Luke does not indicate the exact place where this miracle of integral liberation occurred as he only mentions that: "Now he was teaching in one of the synagogues on the sabbath" (Luke 13:10)—the presence of this slouched woman formed, perhaps, part of the known religious landscape of the days of rest. The body of this woman, deformed by this ailment from which she suffered, was a familiar scene for them and formed part of the traditional "decoration" of the synagogue. Luke does not say anything regarding the name, the age, the occupation, or the family ties of the woman. In the Lucan account it is only specified that for eighteen years she suffered from an ailment that did not allow her to stand up straight (Luke 13:11). The woman's physical condition, according to the Lucan testimony, was quite critical. Even though the account does not mention any specifics regarding the type of illness that caused her distress—it simply records that: "She was bent-over and was quite unable to stand up straight" (Luke 13:11)—without forcing the original meaning of this, it can be affirmed that she had limitations characteristic of her ailment. Walking with a slouch for a relatively long period—almost two decades—had many social, cultural, and familiar disadvantages. Darrell Bock argues that, from the medical point of view, the woman's physical condition can be interpreted as a type of muscular paralysis.[6] Howard Marshall calls this disability a deformation of the spine.[7] But beyond this type of illness that affected the woman's spine, Jesus' action in favor of her made manifest that the moment had arrived to liberate her from this oppression that had converted her into part of the "social waste" of the time due to her condition as a woman and to the ailment from which she suffered.

While Jesus taught in this place, he noticed the presence of this woman who had remained invisible to many passing synagogue attendees. However, Jesus was different. Once he noted her presence in the synagogue, in a gesture that later provoked the heated reaction of the synagogue leader, he displayed a special interest in the critical situation in which the bent-over woman found herself. Luke tells that, "When Jesus saw her, He called her over and said to her, 'Woman, you are freed from your sickness.' And He laid His hands on her" (Luke 13:12–13, NAS). In contrast to the indifference and apathy of the habitual customs of that place, all of which certainly accompanied this woman for many years, Jesus took the initiative in resolving the marginalized woman's drama. The bent-over woman did not ask him for anything at all. She was simply in this public place—perhaps in silence in order not to inconvenience the pious Jews gathered in the synagogue—to see and to hear Jesus. But Jesus, taking the initiative, freed her from all of her oppressions. Following her encounter with him, the woman was totally transformed. She was left free from her sickness, and she was consequently reinserted into society, thus giving account of the liberating dimension of the forgiveness granted by Jesus.[8]

Following Jesus' example, taking the initiative when faced with concrete needs of human beings of flesh and bone demands putting aside indifference and lack of commitment. Seeing what others consider to simply be part of the daily social landscape or a habitual problem about which we should not be shocked means breaking out of the diabolical circle of apathy and complicit silence, and it implies leaving our comfortable position to encounter face to face the daily drama of the destitute and those on the periphery of society. This act results in a direct encounter

---

6. Bock, *Luke*, 241.

7. Marshall, "Luke," 909. Other theologians, following the point of view of A. Rendel Short, think that the bent-over woman's sickness was probably *spondylitis deformans*, an illness in which the bones of the spine fuse together forming a rigid mass (Hendriksen, *Luke*, 699–700; Morris, *Luke*, 244).

8. Senior and Stuhlmueller, *Biblical Foundations for Mission*, 263.

with the forces of the anti-kingdom. In this sense, acting as Jesus did is more than a simple question of theological perspective or political point of view; it demands a public commitment to the defense of human dignity and of the fragile of this time.

IDENTIFICATION WITH THE FRAGILE

According to the Lucan account, Jesus took the initiative to relate with this marginalized woman in a public place. He saw her need and called her (Luke 13:12). Jesus was not that interested in formulating theological questions focused on determining the possible causes of the bent-over woman's sickness. He was interested in solving the problem that had affected the physical and social health of this woman for eighteen years (Luke 13:11, 16). The words he uttered on that occasion demonstrate the special love he had for the marginalized woman: "Woman, you are set free from your ailment" (Luke 13:12). But words were not the only means publicly employed by Jesus to show his interest in the marginalized woman. Jesus' words were accompanied by a very clear gesture of identification with the woman's situation. Luke emphasizes that Jesus "laid his hands on her" (Luke 13:13). By touching the woman with his hands, an unequivocal sign of solidarity with a social outcast, Jesus was valuing the human dignity of this marginalized woman. For Jesus, the bent-over woman was more than a circumstantial fact or an accidental problem he encountered on his way. She was a human being in need of liberation from her ailment, which Jesus identified as a tie or bond of Satan (Luke 13:16).

The words of liberation uttered by Jesus and the compassionate gesture of placing his hands over the ill body had an immediate effect in the woman's life. A bent-over person, for the first time in almost two decades, was able to walk without difficulty: "immediately she stood up straight" (Luke 13:13). The woman was set free from a prolonged ailment and would never again be oppressed by Satan. The first reaction that this fragile and destitute woman had, after being healed by Jesus, was one of gratitude to the Lord for the miracle that he had done in her life. Luke points out that she "began praising God" (Luke 13:13). Jesus' identification with this fragile person, considered at the time as human waste and a social outcast, was accompanied with words and other visible acts of solidarity. This identification with the urgent needs of the defenseless and the underprivileged—with words and actions—outlines the practice of love for neighbor that should be an unmistakable mark of all of the disciples of Jesus of Nazareth.

The account of the bent-over woman liberated by Jesus underlines that compassionate identification with the needs of human beings is correlated with significant changes in the condition of life of the fragile and the defenseless. Identification that leads to commitment expresses itself in words and in visible acts of solidarity, gestures that construct spaces for human communion within which life is valued as a gift of God. But in order to identify with marginalized folk like the bent-over woman, one must cross the bridge that divides the path that we walk on every day; that is, one must cross social and cultural borders that separate human beings. The key word in this process is relocation. The reason is incredibly simple: "Without relocation, without living among the people, without actually becoming one of the people, it is impossible to accurately identify the needs as people perceive them. And once outsiders misdiagnose the problem, their proposed solutions cannot help but miss the mark. They will almost always treat the symptoms without touching the disease."[9]

In other words, we must be conscious that cultural traditions, religious customs, and social prejudices can be large obstacles to relocation. Even more, we must be conscious that religious persons, when they reckon that the worship of tradition is more important than love for neighbor, become intolerant with those who do not mesh with their ideas. Our task as disciples of the crucified and risen Jesus of Nazareth goes beyond cultural conditioning and religious prejudices; it consists of identifying ourselves in word and deed with the fragile and the defenseless of the timeframe in which the God of life has placed us in order to testify to the good news of liberation.

THE GOD OF LIFE

The healing of the bent-over woman did not have the same effect on all those who were present at the synagogue on that occasion. The leader of the synagogue, a place that had the triple purpose of offering education, worship, and government of the civil life of the Jewish community,[10] expressed his disagreement with what took place. But that was not all he

9. Perkins, *With Justice for All*, 64.

10. Feinberg, "Synagogue," 1142–43.

did—he went far beyond that by publicly reprimanding those present and condemning the act of liberation of the bent-over woman as a violation of the sabbath. Luke emphasizes that: "The leader of the synagogue, indignant because Jesus had cured on the sabbath, kept saying to the crowd, 'There are six days on which work ought to be done; come on those days and be cured, and not on the sabbath day'" (Luke 13:14).

The lack of compassion of this zealous guardian of religious traditions can be explained by the legalistic climate of the time, in which the rabbis debated matters like what types of knots could be tied and untied on the day of rest.[11] This religious man could not understand why Jesus had worked—healed—on the day of rest. From his point of view, fed by a theological perspective that had placed human commandments above the will of God regarding the sabbath, God could not heal on the day of rest (Luke 13:14). He believed that God's love was in action only six days of the week; therefore, he classified as an affront to established religious regulations the liberation of this woman and the work God had done. The healing of a person who had been sick for eighteen years did not provoke any feelings of compassion or of joy within the leader of the synagogue. On the contrary, he let his religious prejudices emerge publicly.

But Jesus denounced the hypocrisy of this Jewish leader and others who, like him, had a practice that contradicted their rigid religious principles. Jesus' words to the leader of the synagogue made clear the distance that existed between the legalistic rules and the real conduct of many religious folk: "You hypocrites! Does not each of you on the sabbath untie his ox or his donkey from the manger, and lead it away to give it water?" (Luke 13:15). Jesus' public denunciation was quite clear: if animals could receive basic care on the day of rest, how much more should a human being created in the image of God, a daughter of Abraham whom Satan had enslaved for almost two decades![12]

The biblical text indicates that for the leader of the synagogue and for those who thought like him, the day of rest was a time to preserve traditions, a space to defend established religious regulations, and an occasion to observe human dispositions that limited the action of God to their theological presuppositions. However, for Jesus the day of rest was a day of liberation, an occasion to celebrate the gift of life, a space to proclaim in word and deed the good news of the kingdom of God, a time

11. Marshall, "Luke," 909.

12. Bock, Luke, 241–42.

to unfasten the bonds that oppressed human beings created in the image of God, and an opportune moment to include the excluded. In the words of Norberto Saracco:

> The sabbath institution allows Jesus the opportunity to execute his pedagogical actions. He moves on the imperceptible line which separates the "sacred" from the "profane" and "obedience" from "sin." The actions of Jesus on the sabbath day put to the test the ladder of values of the pharisees and the guardians of the law. His liberating interpretation concerning the observance of the sabbath is assumed to be an attack on the law (Mt. 12:1–14). . . . Jesus did not rebel against the sabbath but rather against the ideological use of the sabbath, which placed the emphasis on tradition rather than on man. In the name of tradition, doctrine, and sanctity, dehumanizing situations are sustained.[13]

In his inaugural discourse in the synagogue of Nazareth, Jesus had expressed the liberating nature of his mission: he had come to preach the favorable year of the Lord (Luke 4:19). This also explains why the healing of the woman on the sabbath, an act criticized by the leader of the synagogue, shows that he—as specified in the programmatic discourse of Nazareth—had been anointed to proclaim liberty to the captives and to set free the oppressed (Luke 4:18).

The compassionate gestures of Jesus in favor of a marginalized person like the bent-over woman expose the dehumanizing religious prejudices and indicate that the needs of a neighbor are more important than love for human traditions. God is life. For this reason, evangelical churches must be spaces for the affirmation and defense of the Life, the worship service a joyful time of celebration of the Life, actions of service social channels through which the love of God continually flows, expressing itself in concrete gestures of compassion, solidarity, and comradeship. Evangelical churches must be inclusive communities, places where all are treated as human beings created in the image of God, and spaces where the Life is loved and defended.

AN INTEGRAL LIBERATION

According to the Lucan testimony, this woman who could not stand up straight in any way had for eighteen years had a spirit of sickness (Luke

13. Saracco, "Liberating Options of Jesus," 36.

13:11). This first mention of the physical problem that affected her is explained more when Jesus declares that the illness had been induced by Satan (Luke 13:16). The oppression of the woman was not only physical. The situation she was in was quite delicate, and for this reason, she needed to be freed from the problem that was oppressing her. The physical condition of the woman, her prolonged illness, reveals to what extent Satan oppresses and enslaves human beings. In fact, the woman could not stand up; the deformation she had in her spine did not permit her to walk normally. David Gooding, commenting on this woman's situation, underlines that her illness "was not due simply to physical causes."[14] Regarding this same topic, Howard Marshall points out that, "Human suffering is due to the same cosmic power as human sin."[15] Darrell Bock, meanwhile, argues that, "The mention of the spirit is important, because the woman's opponent is not merely mortality or the natural process of aging but a spiritual agent. The age of her condition indicates how serious it is."[16]

Faced with this situation, calling the woman, Jesus said to this excluded person, "Woman, you are set free from your ailment" (Luke 13:12). When the leader of the synagogue reacts angrily to the miracle carried out in this woman's life, according to him a violation of the sabbath, Jesus responds by affirming that she was also a daughter of the promise, a descendent of Abraham, the friend of God (Luke 13:12, 16). With this unequivocal gesture of love, seasoned with words and concrete gestures of solidarity, Jesus clearly expressed that he had come to free persons oppressed by Satan. In this sense, Jesus' actions on the day of rest show that the sabbath was an appropriate time to reveal the impotence of Satan. The liberating mission of Jesus was made manifest. He is the Lord of life.

Jesus' disciples should be aware that Satan still continues to oppress people. In this time of accelerated change they must remember that the purpose of God is to free human beings from every bond and every form of slavery. They should never forget that churches are called to proclaim at all times the good news of liberation in the name of Jesus. Words and acts of compassion must be daily signs of the people of God in mission. Religious traditions and social prejudices often generate attitudes of intolerance and dehumanizing situations. They cloud vision and do not permit

14. Gooding, *According to Luke*, 253.

15. Marshall, "Luke," 909.

16. Bock, *Luke*, 241.

seeing beyond what has been established by cultural patterns. This situation explains why it will always be a scandal to transgress religious dispositions that limit God's action. It will never be easy to take the initiative to break the bonds of oppression and generate changes in the mentality of persons. But identification with the concrete needs of the oppressed, this identification whose correlate is an irrevocable commitment, has as its goal the integral liberation of human beings of flesh and bone. In this sense, churches must be communities where life is affirmed and defended, not mere social groups characterized by human traditions that limit the sovereignty of God. The worship service must be a space for celebration of God's love, a time to proclaim liberation from every bond, and a moment to confess that God is the God of life. Only in this way can churches be channels of reconciliation, instruments to proclaim the forgiveness of sins in the name of Jesus, and vehicles of service to all human beings and communities where the justice of God is present at every moment.

7

Let the Children Come to Me

Jesus of Nazareth and the Scorned of Society

Luke 18:15–17

INTRODUCTION

One of the overarching themes in Luke's gospel is God's special love for the poor and the excluded, among them children. In the cultural world of the first century, children were on the periphery of society. They were considered as insignificant and even as incomplete human beings.[1] According to the Lucan testimony, when Jesus began to proclaim the good news of the kingdom of God, he related with the defenseless and helpless social sectors, like children. "Jesus placed special importance on receiving with kindness and hospitality the least important members of

---

1. Gutiérrez, *God of Life*, 114; France, *Matthew*, 283–84; Morris, *Luke*, 192.

society."[2] From his point of view, they were also subjects of his love and, therefore, beneficiaries of the message of salvation that he proclaimed. He publicly declared that children could also be citizens of the kingdom of God. Luke records this in his gospel (Luke 18:15–17).[3] The other synoptic gospels do as well (Matt 19:13–15; Mark 10:13–16). But adults do not always value and treat children as human beings created in the image of God. Sometimes we value and treat them as insignificant and as hindrances. Jesus' disciples acted in this way as well on one occasion. They valued and treated them as disturbances to the Teacher and thought that it was not worth dedicating a little time to attend to them (Matt 19:13; Mark 10:13; Luke 18:15).

One of the biblical texts key to knowing how Jesus related with children is Luke 18:15–17 (cf. Matt 19:13–15; Mark 10:13–16). In this biblical text one can clearly observe a contrast in attitudes toward children, capturing, on one hand, the way Jesus valued and treated them in this moment, and, on the other hand, the way his disciples did. There is no point of contact between these two attitudes. Luke and the other synoptic gospels underline that Jesus had a distinct way of relating to children, quite distinct from the inconsiderate and unfriendly attitude of his disciples. Jesus always had time for children. He did not see them as his disciples saw them, as Jesus valued and treated them as human beings, while his disciples valued and treated them as mere hindrances. Jesus thus teaches us a distinct way to value and treat children, a lesson that is highly relevant in this time in which the excluded, defenseless, and fragile social sectors are confined to the basement of human relations and only count as cold numbers on statistical charts that graph the levels of poverty and extreme poverty in which millions of human beings find themselves. The way Jesus of Nazareth saw, valued, and treated the fragile of society, rather than an interesting theological fact or an ingredient for academic discussion, is outlined as a strong wake-up call to all those who see, value, and treat the excluded and the defenseless as mere social scraps.

2. Barton, "Child, Children," 102.

3. Luke also records in his gospel other cases in which Jesus' special love for children is emphasized. One of them is the case of the resurrection of the only daughter of Jairus (Luke 8:40–42, 49–56). The other case is the account of the disciples' discussion regarding who among them would be the greatest (Luke 9:46–48). Although we do not know the exact ages of the only son of the widow from Nain (Luke 7:11–17) or of the demon-possessed boy who was liberated by Jesus (Luke 9:37–43), it is probable that they were also minors.

THE INDIGNATION OF JESUS

The different points of view that Jesus of Nazareth and his disciples had regarding the place of children in God's purpose is one of the themes present in Luke 18:15–17. There it is emphasized that Jesus' attitude was radically different than the attitude of the disciples when faced with the desire of parents or close relatives to have their children receive the Teacher's blessing. In his account Luke tells that, "People were even bringing infants to him that he might touch them" (Luke 18:15). Matthew, meanwhile, mentions the following: "Then little children were being brought to him in order that he might lay his hands on them and pray" (Matt 19:13). According to the gospel of Mark, "People were bringing little children to him in order that he might touch them" (Mark 10:13). There was nothing strange about this desire of the parents and relatives, as it was a common practice of the time for children to receive the blessing of elders and for the elders to pray for them.[4] And, of course, the gospels indicate that Jesus received them without any problem or inconvenience. But the disciples had an attitude different than that of their Teacher. According to Saint Luke, "When the disciples saw it, they sternly ordered them not to do it" (Luke 18:15). Mark expresses that "the disciples spoke sternly to them" (Mark 10:13). Meanwhile, Matthew's gospel makes this useful specification: "The disciples spoke sternly to those who brought them" (Matt 19:13). This indicates that the reprobation or rebuke of the disciples was not directed at the children as Luke and Mark appear to suggest, but at the parents or close relatives of the children. What is thus clear, if one takes into account the unanimous way the synoptic gospels tell of this event, is that the disciples rebuked or condemned the action of the adults.[5]

Why did Jesus' disciples react in this way? The way they treated the parents and relatives of the children indicates that for them, perhaps, it was a waste of time for Jesus to dedicate himself to attending to the needs of the insignificant.[6] In other words, their attitude revealed that for them, like for many Jews of their time, children lacked value and formed part of those who were considered disposable. According to Roy Zuck, "Jesus' disciples may have thought that his praying for children was insignificant

---

4. France, *Matthew*, 283; Morris, *Luke*, 291.

5. Mark uses the Greek word *epitimao*, which means to condemn, reprimand, or threaten.

6. France, *Matthew*, 283; Morris, *Luke*, 291.

compared with his other important ministries such as teaching and heal-ing, or that he was too busy or tired to be bothered with anyone other than adults. Or they may have supposed children were too young to ben-efit from his attention."[7]

For the disciples, who were conditioned by the predominant mental-ity of their time, children were confined to the periphery.[8] However, for Jesus, children were important and had value as human beings created in the image of God. This explains why he saw, valued, and treated them as human beings with dignity. The contrast between the two perspectives is clear. Moreover, when Jesus realized that the disciples had rebuked or condemned those bringing the children, according to Mark's account he became indignant (Mark 10:14). The word *aganaktéo* (to become indig-nant or angry) is a verb that expresses a strong sense of indignation. Why did Jesus become indignant? Undoubtedly, he became indignant because for him, in contrast to the disciples, the kingdom of God was also accessi-ble to children. In light of this event, it can be affirmed that God takes care of all, including children, as the kingdom of God is not just for adults.[9] In God's eyes, no one is less important. Jesus' indignation indicates thus. But it is also an indignation that summons us to change our way of seeing, valuing, and treating children. Jesus' indignation challenges us to examine our motivations in our relations with our neighbors. It also demands a concrete commitment to urgent tasks like the defense of the defenseless and of the fragile of society. This is the case because the historic vocation of Jesus' disciples is not to be like others, but to be distinct from non-Christians, both in their way of thinking and in their life practice.

CHILDREN AND THE KINGDOM OF GOD

Children and the kingdom of God is another theme emphasized in Luke 18:15–17. The central idea seems to be the demand of a change in mental-ity regarding the way of relating with defenseless and dependent social sectors like children and, therefore, the inversion of values that is cor-related with the proclamation of the kingdom of God. The words Jesus

7. Zuck, *Precious in His Sight*, 12.

8. In the patriarchal society of that time, children were under the care of adults and occupied the lowest rung of the social structure. They formed part of the world of the excluded and the helpless of society.

9. Bock, *Luke*, 298.

voiced on this occasion, according to Luke, were the following: "Let the little children come to me, and do not stop them; for it is to such as these that the kingdom of God belongs. Truly I tell you, whoever does not receive the kingdom of God as a little child will never enter it" (Luke 18:16–17). Mark records the same information as Luke (Mark 10:14). Matthew includes only the first part recorded by Luke and Mark, using the phrase "kingdom of heaven" in place of "kingdom of God" (Matt 19:14). What is the significance and what are the implications of these words of Jesus that the synoptic gospels, especially Luke, record?

Jesus' affirmation, "Let the little children come to me, and do not stop them; for it is to such as these that the kingdom of God belongs" (Luke 18:16; cf. Matt 19:14; Mark 10:14), indicates that the message of salvation is also for them. In this way, the inclusivity of mission emphasized in Luke also has an effect on defenseless and fragile human sectors like children. Perhaps this explains why Luke uses the formula *prosepheron de auto kai ta brephe* or "people were bringing even infants to him" (Luke 18:15), thus underlining that even children of tender age were brought so that Jesus might bless them. Both the word *paidion* ("little children" as in Luke 18:16–17) and the term *brephos* ("infants" or "small children" as in Luke 18:15) clearly establish that Jesus was referring to children of flesh and bone and to concrete human beings.[10] The same idea is present also in the gospels of Mark (10:13) and Matthew (19:13), as both gospels use the word *paidion* (little children), which refers to children who must be carried by individuals larger than themselves. The information in the gospels leads to establish, then, that children of all ages are beneficiaries of the kingdom. And it should not be forgotten that the *paidion* formed part of the world of the defenseless in the Jewish cultural climate of the first century,[11] and that they were considered as incomplete beings and as unimportant, together with the poor, women, and the sick.[12]

The other idea present in the accounts of Luke (v. 18:17) and Mark (v. 10:15), but not in that of Matthew, is that access to the kingdom of God does not depend on human effort. What is needed to have access to the kingdom, however, relates to how children were considered in the cultural world of the first century and not necessarily to docility

10. Luke uses the word *brephos* (infants or small children) five times in his gospel (Luke 1:41, 44; 2:12, 16; 18:15). The other gospels do not use this word.

11. Zuck, *Precious in His Sight*, 206; Strange, *Children in the Early Church*, 48, 51, 64.

12. Gutiérrez, *God of Life*, 114.

and infantile trust.[13] In other words, it relates to the conditions of dependency, insignificance, and fragility that were associated with children according to the cultural patterns of the time.[14] Thus, to become part of the kingdom community, one must accept his or her condition of dependency, insignificance, and fragility before God.[15] Jesus thus used the way that children were assessed in the first century as a visual metaphor to underline pedagogically how to enter the kingdom and how the benefits of salvation can be obtained.[16] As H. R. Weber notes, "Already Mark, Matthew and Luke seem to have been more interested in what a child symbolizes than in Jesus' attitude to actual children."[17]

Jesus' words "as a little child" (Mark 10:15; Luke 18:17) do not refer to the age or the stature of children. The reference is to their condition in the exclusive society of the time.[18] Jesus inverts, therefore, the way access to positions of preeminence and dominance was assessed at the time. Entrance into the kingdom of God does not have any connection to the mundane idea of the conquest of power or of becoming and being great in predominant society. Entrance into the kingdom demands assuming the condition of a child, of a helpless person, of a defenseless person, of someone who is not valued in society. This is the case because Jesus'

13. Gutiérrez, *God of Life*, 114.

14. Escudero Freire, *Devolver el Evangelio*, 213.

15. Gustavo Gutiérrez specifies that: "When the Lord cautions his disciples: 'Let the children come to me . . . for the kingdom of heaven belongs to such as these' (Mt 19:14), we quickly think of the docility and trustfulness of children. If we do, we fail to see how radical the message of Jesus is. In the cultural world of Judaism at that time, children were regarded as incomplete human beings; . . . they were counted among the unimportant folk. . . . To be 'such as these,' like children, meant therefore to be insignificant, to be someone on whom society set no value" (*God of Life*, 114).

16. William Hendriksen holds that: "Jesus is talking about the simple, humble, unquestioning, trustful manner in which a child accepts what is offered to him" (Hendriksen, *Mark*, 383). Roy Zuck specifies the following: "A child recognizes his lowly, helpless condition, he knows he is insignificant, small, and totally dependent. God's kingdom is not achieved by human effort; 'it must be received as God's gift through simple trust by those who acknowledge their inability to gain it any other way'" (*Precious in His Sight*, 214).

17. Cited in Barton, "Child, Children," 101.

18. One author points out that, "The sentences in the gospels about children and those who are like them confirm the kind of predilection Jesus had for the poor, the unsophisticated folk, the weak of this world. . . . Those who are like children are, then, the poor, the insignificant, the defenseless, those without voice and without influence" (Escudero, *Devolver el Evangelio*, 213–14, my translation).

words must be interpreted in light of the cultural context in which he uttered them. And in the Jewish cultural world of the first century, children depended completely on adults and were considered as socially inferior. What is emphasized, therefore, is their condition of insignificance and dependence.[19] The kingdom of God should be received like a child (*hos paidion*). This is what the synoptic gospels unanimously indicate (Matt 18:3; Mark 10:15; Luke 18:17).

To enter into the kingdom of God one must be like a child, that is, assume the condition of orphanhood, of dependence, and of insignificance. But this also signifies that Jesus sees, values, and treats the weak, the unprotected, and the "nobodies" as human beings. Thus, from Jesus' perspective, a child is just as important as an adult and entrance into the kingdom does not depend on things like status or capacity to exercise power and dominion over others. The new community knows no borders. The good news of salvation is accessible to all, including the vulnerable and insignificant like children. Children have a legitimate place in Christian community.

THE GESTURES OF JESUS

Jesus expressed his love for human beings in multiple ways. He used both spoken language and the language of gestures to express his solidarity with the destitute and the insignificant. Be it through words or through gestures, Jesus' intention was to integrally free the defenseless and the dispossessed, the distressed and the needy, the ragged and the social outcasts. The passages narrating the occasion in which parents and close relatives brought children so that Jesus might bless them and pray for them highlight three concrete gestures of love for the children carried out by Jesus. Luke indicates the following: "But Jesus called for them. . ." (Luke 18:16). Matthew, whose explanation is more complete than the other synoptic gospels, states that, "Then little children were being brought to him in order that he might lay his hands on them and pray" (Matt 19:13); it

---

19. Citing a portion of the book *Les Béatitudes II* (Dupont, 181), Carlos Escudero Freire states the following to reinforce his argument that the phrase "like a child" in Luke 18:17 and Mark 10:15 refers to the condition of weakness and of insignificance that they had in the first century: "The true foundation of the promise is not found, as we believe, in the practice of a virtue, but in God's predilection for all that is small, for all that does not have value in the eyes of the world: it is the predilection that the poor share with the children" (*Devolver el Evangelio*, 215, my translation).

also points out that Jesus "laid his hands on them and went on his way" (Matt 19:15). And Mark is the only one to mention that Jesus "took them up in his arms, laid his hands on them, and blessed them" (Mark 10:16). What were Jesus' gestures of love?

First, according to the Lucan account and the emphasis mentioned there, it can be inferred that Jesus had a particular interest in children. Thus, while the disciples rebuked the attitude of those bringing the children so that he might bless them and pray for them, Jesus called them, thereby showing that the defenseless and the helpless were important to him (Luke 18:16). Jesus' indignation, when he became aware of the conduct of his disciples (Mark 10:14), also constitutes a clear indicator of the value that children had for Jesus and of his special concern for the insignificant and the weak of society.

Second, the gospels of Matthew and Mark point out that Jesus took the children in his arms or picked them up (Mark 10:16) and laid his hands on them to pray and to bless them (Matt 19:13, 15; Mark 10:16). Both of Jesus' visible and public gestures, holding the children in his arms and laying his hands on them, constitute unconcealed signs of solidarity with the defenseless and the helpless. Moreover, they were two visible forms of affection aimed at reversing the destiny of the excluded and of the insignificant. Jesus valued and treated children as what they already were: human beings created in the image of God. By taking them in his arms and laying his hands on them, he identified with their condition and became one of them. He did not act as the disciples did in that moment. Jesus did not allow social or cultural prejudices that characterized the Jewish world of the first century to prevail over the commandment to love one's neighbor and to annul the liberating effects of the message of salvation he proclaimed.

Third, according to the testimony of Mark, Jesus "took them up in his arms, laid his hands on them, and blessed them" (Mark 10:16). The idea transmitted in Mark's account is that Jesus gently blessed, one by one, all of the children. It was not a waste of time to take them in his arms, lay hands on each one of them, and bless them one by one. For Jesus children were so important that he devoted the necessary time to show, through word and deed, that they were also recipients of the good news of liberation. This explains why he took them in his arms, laid his hands on them, and blessed them. This same attitude and practice must be a distinctive mark of Christian churches in their relation to the defenseless and in their practice of defending the human dignity of the weak and the insignificant.

Christian churches must take interest in children, not as objects of work or as pretexts to obtain economic support, but as subjects, as human beings with dignity, and as persons of flesh and bone who need to be confronted with the liberating message of the kingdom of God. This will demand, of course, an examination of motivations for social service and of work strategies that are derived from these motivations. God has a special preference for children. In this sense, defending a marginalized person and losing face for the defenseless are concrete ways of expressing a genuine commitment to the God of life. Jesus invites us to break the vicious cycle of indifference and to come out of our "protective bubble" with which we intend to ignore the grim reality of children who are ill-treated and condemned to die at a slow pace in the dumps of history. Consequently, we must radically change our mentality (our theological perspective), and adopt a new lifestyle marked by the values of the kingdom of God (love in action). We must get actively involved in an integral ministry that has the goal of defending the human dignity of the insignificant and the destitute, who are also created in the image of God.

Our missional horizons must be extended. The tasks of prevention, protection, rehabilitation, and consolation are necessary. But we must look further. In our work schedule there must be room for the promotion and defense of the human dignity of the destitute. This demands passing from immediate or conjectural social service to collective social actions aimed at the integral transformation of the living conditions of all those excluded by the system. This requires knowing the channels of legal and paralegal dispute that contribute to this purpose. It is also necessary to know the mechanisms of political work, to understand how the justice administration system works, to be familiar with the international instruments for the protection and defense of children, and to understand that our network of relations must be more inclusive. Will we be available to speak loudly for those who have no voice in today's globalized world?

8

Surrendering One's Life as an Offering

A Theological Proposition from the World of the Poor

Luke 21:1–4

INTRODUCTION

Women, Samaritans, tax collectors, lepers, children, and those ill in any way formed part of the world of the excluded when Jesus of Nazareth began to travel through the towns and villages of the marginal region of Galilee proclaiming the good news of the kingdom of God. Each of these fragile and vulnerable sectors was considered as the disposables or the "nobodies" of society. Even more, in the patriarchal cultural climate of the first century, social and religious prejudices had turned into socially accepted effective vehicles for excluding those who were classified as less important. This particular reality explains why the way Jesus of Nazareth publicly related with women, one of the human sectors condemned to social ostracism, involved calling into question the cultural patterns of his time. This unusual action stands out even more when one takes into account that the carpenter from Nazareth had among his disciples several women from the spurned region of Galilee (Luke 8:1–3; 23:49, 55). Regarding this, Gustavo Gutiérrez points out that:

> The attitude of Jesus to women represented . . . a real break . . . with the dominant categories of his time. His behavior elicited reactions of surprise and even scandal among his contemporaries, including his own disciples. . . . The mere fact that women collaborated with Jesus shows how new and different his attitude to them was. But this only fed the prejudices and hostility of those who felt threatened by the ministry of the Galilean preacher.[1]

The third gospel notably emphasizes the way Jesus of Nazareth, breaking with the exclusive cultural patterns of his time, had a special concern for the social sectors that were on the periphery of society, such as women. Luke is the gospel most favorable to this marginalized and excluded social sector.[2] Throughout his gospel, when he records the missionary work of the teacher from Galilee, Luke highlights this distinct aspect of Jesus' liberating mission (Luke 4:38–39; 7:11–17, 36–50; 8:2–3, 40–56; 10:38–42; 11:27–28; 13:10–17; 21:1–4; 23:26—24:12). From the first chapters of the gospel, the outstanding role of women in the history of salvation is emphasized. This is confirmed by the cases of Elizabeth (1:39–45), the Virgin Mary (1:26–38, 46–56), and the prophetess Anna (2:36–38). Moreover, two of the exclusively Lucan parables have women as the central characters (Luke 15:8–10; 18:1–8). All of this indicates that, more than any other gospel writer, Luke stresses Jesus' association with and treatment of women, thus knocking down, to the shock of all, a social and religious barrier imposed by the patriarchal society of his time.[3]

The stories concerning how Jesus valued the generosity of the sinful woman in the house of Simon the Pharisee (Luke 7:36–50) and regarding how he integrally liberated the bent over woman (Luke 13:10–17) have a special connotation in light of the Lucan perspective of the liberating mission of Jesus. However, the account of the poor widow's offering, recorded by Luke in his gospel and also found in the gospel of Mark (12:41–44),

---

1. Gutiérrez, *God of Life*, 168.

2. Ryan, "Women from Galilee," 56.

3. Senior and Stuhlmueller, *Biblical Foundations for Mission*, 261.

has a unique theological tint as it combines several elements that articulate the liberating mission of Jesus. This triply excluded woman—due to her position as a woman, a widow, and a poor person—who is described as a very poor widow, represents a paradigm of absolute trust in the will of God.[4] The generous and trusting attitude of this very poor woman—an absolute surrender to the God of life—did not go unnoticed by Jesus (Luke 21:1–4; Mark 12:41–44). The account of the spiritual experience of the very poor widow emphasizes her generosity that expressed itself in the voluntary renunciation of all that she had at the moment for her sustenance, thus publicly showing her surrender without reservations to the God of life and her full trust in the care of her Heavenly Father. The lesson underlined in the experience of the poor widow is that the essence of true offering is sacrifice, thus pointing out that the value lies not in the quantity of money one gives, but rather in how one is giving. In the words of Yoder, "The quantity of money that one gives is of little importance. What is important is what one gives. If it is a part of one's income, then this is not righteousness, goodness, and good faith. If it is capital that one gives then everything is in order."[5]

The story of the extremely poor widow's offering emphasizes that God knows the deepest motives of human beings and draws attention to the fact that he values what one gives with true sacrifice and generosity, and not what is offered without sacrifice, due to custom, to good appearances, or out of mere convenience.

A CLASH OF THEOLOGIES

Two theological perspectives on God, two ways of relating with him and confessing him publicly, were revealed when the rich gave an offering out of their excess and the very poor widow deposited in the offering coffer all that she had. This woman's condition of widowhood was already in itself an enormous disadvantage—on top of being a woman, which made her culturally, socially, and religiously marginalized—in the patriarchal society of the time in which widows did not have many possibilities for work to earn a living. But she was not merely a woman and a widow. According to the Lucan account, she was also a *penichros* (very poor, needy or unhappy,

---

4. The third gospel also mentions other widows who received special attention from Jesus (Luke 7:11–17; 18:3, 5; 20:47).

5. Yoder, *Politics of Jesus*, 76.

as is indicated in Luke 21:2) and a *ptōchos* (poor, stooped, frightened, and destitute person who must beg for a living, as stated in Luke 21:3), who out of her *hysterēma* (poverty, lack, scarcity, need, or deficiency, as pointed out in Luke 21:4) offered all that she needed, all that she had to live on.[6] The differences—social, cultural, economic, and theological—between the rich and the very poor widow are quite obvious. Jesus' words regarding the value of the widow's offering—"this poor widow has put in more than all of them" (Luke 21:3)—situated in the context of the prior denunciation of the hypocrisy of the religious who, according to Jesus, devoured the houses of widows (Luke 20:46–47), thus depreciating the Old Testament teaching that presented God as the defender of widows (Ps 68:5) and demanded that they be protected (Isa 1:17), express a clear concern for the human dignity of this woman, who was marginalized and considered as a "nobody" according to the predominant cultural categories of the time.

An analysis of Luke 21:1–4 indicates that the problem of the economically powerful, similar to that of the hypocritical scribes (Luke 20:45–47), was the superficiality of their religious actions. Both the scribes and the rich had a deficit of coherency between their theological discourse concerning God and their concrete practice. Jesus was not impressed by the appearance of their piety, by the mask of their religious faith, nor by the quantity of money that the rich deposited into the treasury. Jesus saw and valued what others, impressed by the apparent generosity of the rich, failed to capture: the generosity of a poor widow expressed in the act of offering two insignificant coins that were all she had to live on, something others probably spurned. Jesus does not look at the ostentation of religious acts, but rather the heart of individuals. Thus, while for the rich God was simply a part of the spiritual landscape of the time and a good pretext for controlling political and religious power, for the very poor widow he was the God of life to whom she had to give her life as an offering. Does not the same occur today in this time of the emergence of religion in public life? The very poor widow was not a theologian like the scribes, trained for casuistry and for deliberating intricate religious regulations, but the poor widow's implicit theology emerged when she gave as her offering all that she had for her sustenance. For the rich God was merely a theological theme and their spirituality was limited to private ethics. For the very

---

6. Luke is the only one to use the word *penicrós* (Luke 21:2). This word is not used in any other New Testament document.

poor widow God was the sustenance of her life and her spirituality had a public reach and effect. This is so, because with her gesture of generosity and of total abandonment in the hands of God, she was confessing that God was her *go'el*, the defender of widows and the one who would lose face for the defenseless, the God of life who took care of all those whom society treated as social waste and as human scum. From the widow's theological perspective, God was not only the Lord of the private sphere of life, but the sovereign God who had in his hands control of all things and therefore could provide for her. For her God was not the property of the rich, neither had he been kidnapped by those who wield power in the world; rather, he was the defender of widows and of all those who society classified as disposable dross (Deut 10:17–18; Pss 68:5; 146:9).

APPEARANCES DECEIVE

The scene is situated "in the temple, the heart of religious, economic, and political power in Jerusalem."[7] According to the version in Mark's gospel, while Jesus was sitting "down opposite the treasury" (Mark 12:41), probably close to the women's court where the treasury was located, he "watched the crowd putting money into the treasury" (Mark 12:41).[8] In his version of this incident, Luke stresses that Jesus "looked up and saw rich people putting their gifts into the treasury; he also saw a poor widow put in two small copper coins" (Luke 21:1–2). The substantial difference between the offering of the rich and the offering of the poor widow was not in the quantity of coins that they deposited into the treasury, as there was nothing wrong with the act of offering itself. The difference, however, was in how they were giving the offering to God, because there is a notable difference between giving out of our surplus and giving in a sacrificial way that affects our security and economic stability. The biblical account underlines that for the rich, whose security and economic stability were not at risk, it was a mere contribution that formed part of their religious activism. But for the poor widow it was a total sacrifice,[9] particularly because, "She gave all that she possessed, all that she needed

---

7. Gutiérrez, *God of Life*, 113.

8. William Hendriksen holds that, "We must picture Jesus as being seated somewhere in the Women's Court, with its thirteen trumpet-shaped chests, that is, receptacles for gifts and dues" (*Luke*, 919).

9. Cole, *Mark*, 271.

to sustain her life, which, in the perspective of the poor, generally covers what one needs for the present day."[10] And this gesture of generosity expressed or made public a spirituality that had as one of its pillars the confession of God as the God of life.

The Lucan account underlines that among so many people who deposited their offerings in the Jerusalem Temple that day, Jesus fixed his gaze on a very poor widow (Luke 21:1–2). Beyond the apparent insignificance of her offering, he valued the texture of this marginalized and excluded widow's authentic faith: "Truly, I tell you, this poor widow has put in more than all of them" (Luke 21:3). The phrase "has put in more than all of them" indicates that the two small coins that the poor widow gave as an offering were worth much more than the money that all of the rich had deposited because they had given out of their excess (Luke 21:4). Jesus sees what we frequently overlook or wrongly judge. Jesus examines the heart. He does not see appearances or the religious masks of people. He differentiates between hypocrisy and true devotion to God. Jesus' scrutinizing gaze is not the common gaze that concentrates on the epidermis or on the surface of things, that very human action that so frequently is impressed by external acts that often hide true motivations. Jesus' gaze examines intentions and reveals hidden interests that at a glance are not easily distinguished. Jesus sees the heart and not the false religious acts or the masks of apparent piety. Appearances deceive. But Jesus distinguished between the apparent and the real, between the superficial and the authentic, between the external side of things and the internal things of the heart. He was not like we who too frequently only see what leaves an impression, what works, the ephemeral, the circumstantial, the worldly, the material.

As disciples of Jesus in the globalized world in which people of all ages and economic positions are socialized to be concerned with the accumulation of material goods in the shortest time possible, we need to see beyond appearances so that we do not let the values of predominant society be those that profile our lifestyles and determine our daily agendas. At this particular juncture in which many adopt as the slogan for their existence the formula "I consume therefore I am" or "I buy therefore I am," Jesus' warning regarding inordinate attachment to worldly things has special relevance for us: "one's life does not consist in the abundance of possessions" (Luke 12:15). Let us not forget then, as popular wisdom

10. Gnilka, *Evangelio Según San Marcos*, vol. II, 208, my translation.

states, that appearances can be deceiving. Appearances on occasion have a religious disguise, a cloak of piety or a mask of generosity, as in the case of the rich who gave out of their excess. Jesus challenges us to abandon the life based on appearances and take on a lifestyle founded in a total surrender to the God of life.

TRUE SACRIFICE

The act of giving up all of the material resources she had at the moment —two trivial coins according to human criteria—expresses that, in contrast to the rich who had a tailor-made god of adornment, for this poor widow God was the center of her life. The theological perception of this triply excluded woman explains why she voluntarily renounced her possessions, all that she had to live on. A pair of coins of scant value on the exchange market of the time, two pieces of metal that together amounted to a small fraction of any currency of the lowest value of today,[11] expressed, however, a concrete gesture of total dependence on God. This very poor woman gave sacrificially, with absolute detachment, with extreme generosity. For this reason, "In the sight of Jesus her gift was the greatest, for what God measures is not so much the size of the gift as what remains after it has been given. In this particular case the donor had given her whole income."[12]

The poor widow could have legitimately kept one of the coins for her daily sustenance, for it formed part of her property. By giving one of the coins, she would have been giving half of her possessions or 50 percent of what she had. But she gave up as an offering to God all of her capital, all that she had to survive on, all that could guarantee her sustenance. By giving all that she had, she was risking her future, putting it in the hands of God, depending only on the mercy of the Heavenly Father. In spite of her extreme poverty, she kept nothing for herself, and by that action she publicly confessed that her entire life, present and future, was in the hands of the God of life. This explains why Jesus valued this widow's gesture. As Gutiérrez points out:

> In the eyes of this acute observer who looks beyond appearances, this is not an everyday event. He reads reality in light of the message about the kingdom that he himself proclaims. The master

11. Hendriksen, *Mark*, 506–7.

12. Marshall, "Luke," 919.

then shows his disciples the meaning of what is happening. The widow's action seems insignificant to eyes not illuminated by faith, but in Jesus' eyes her alms are worth more than that of the ostentatious rich, who give only of their surplus. For the widow gives what is in fact necessary for her livelihood.[13]

The lesson to be derived from the poor widow's example is quite clear. Some offer out of their excess, without sacrifice, without putting their economic stability at risk, without altering their living budget, without risking anything, keeping for themselves more than what they need to live on each day. Others, like the poor widow, offer sacrificially and present themselves as an offering to God. Their security does not lie in the "money god," neither does their happiness lie in the mere accumulation of material goods. What they are, human beings created in the image of God whose dignity is an inalienable gift of the Creator, does not depend on what they have or on the mere accumulation of material goods. Rather, what they have neither defines identity nor their place in society, and because of this, they are open to renouncing all exaggerated attachment to worldly things.

Giving sacrificially, voluntarily renouncing excessive attachment to fleeting things, demands recognizing that our daily bread—as affirmed in the Lord's Prayer (Matt 6:9–13)—comes from God and that our whole life is in his hands. Giving sacrificially involves, moreover, putting aside what it means for many to make a name for themselves and to preserve their image of a prosperous person in an environment that grows more competitive and exclusive every day. It is not a lack of sound judgment or of foresight. It is presenting all that we have—ourselves—as an offering to God, thus expressing a surrender without reservations and without conditions to God's sovereign will. The obedient and yielding attitude of the poor widow is a clear example of this.

THE GOD OF LIFE

The poor widow casted in all that she had to live on. She kept nothing for herself. By giving all that she had at the moment, through that gesture of absolute trust in the Lord's provision, she publicly confessed God as Father and glorified his name by presenting herself as an offering. For this poor, spurned, and oppressed woman, God was the foundation of her

13. Gutiérrez, God of Life, 113.

life. And, for this reason, she gave what was essential for her.[14] More than offering two coins of meager value, all of her capital or all of her material possessions, the widow was giving up her life as an offering. Who was going to fight for her material needs? Why did she give everything to God? Why did she not keep one of the coins she had for herself? Luke underlines in his account that she trusted her whole life to the sovereign will of the Lord. The surrender of the most precious thing she had at the moment, two small coins, was a concrete sign of absolute submission to the Lord. In this poor widow's act of extreme generosity, it was revealed that when she gave all her money as an offering, it was a public confession of God as Father and as protector of her life. For this poor woman, in contrast to the rich, God was much more important than money. This theological understanding manifested itself in the generous act of giving sacrificially. For her God was the God of life. In other words, this excluded woman condemned to social ostracism, according to the cultural patterns of the time, publicly confessed that God occupied the center or the place of priority in her life. The situation of material poverty in which she found herself did not turn her into a selfish person who only thought of her own wellbeing. She had learned that love for God comes before love for the "god" of money.

This widow, who Jesus used as a model of true generosity, with her sacrificial gesture of generosity, showed the route that every disciple of Jesus of Nazareth is called to follow. This woman's gesture of sacrificial love revealed the texture of her faith in God, whom she confessed as the God of life. Consequently, this widow's practice of faith, a visible gesture recognized by Jesus himself, indicates that God does not expect only material possessions as an offering, but also life itself. In this sense, "God's assessment of the poor [like the widow] must spur on the community to not only accept the example of the widow, but to be at the side of those abandoned like her."[15]

But generosity is not exactly a frequent practice in this time in which exaggerated attachment to material goods and the lethal virus of individualism seem to impose themselves as life models or paradigms. Within this exclusive reality, the proposition of a lifestyle marked by sacrifice, solidarity, and commitment to the excluded proves to be quite strange and is considered a passé subject or a mere religious theme fit only for the

14. Ibid.

15. Gnilka, *Evangelio Según San Marcos*, vol. II, 208, my translation.

misled or naïve. People do not seem to realize that precisely in sacrifice, solidarity, and commitment is the seed of a new society in which all will be valued and treated as human beings of flesh and bone created in the image of God, and not as mere pieces of the invisible hand of the market or as disposable articles in today's globalized world. Selfishness, the desire to accumulate for oneself, expresses not only a lack of love for neighbor, but also a life practice in which love for material goods is above any other social or religious commitment. However, beyond the selfishness that grazes in all social circles and all cultural frameworks in which generosity is a word outside of their vocabulary and an unnecessary practice, for the disciples of the crucified and risen Lord, gospel obedience demands renouncing all exaggerated attachment to worldly goods and presenting our lives as an offering to God. The example of the very poor widow sketched the route that the disciples of Jesus of Nazareth must travel at all times and in all historical circumstances.

9

But Not So with You

Jesus of Nazareth and Political Power

Luke 22:24–27

INTRODUCTION

One of the most well known things that has characterized the Latin American Protestant religious camp in the last decade has been the eruption of citizens of evangelical confession onto the public stage. A preliminary analysis of this new phenomenon in regional political history shows that the public conduct of a high percentage of those who made incursions into the parliamentary confines and into the terrain of the local governments was not really distinct from that of the customary characters in this world, for evangelicals also acted like "normal" politicians for whom figuration and opportunism are daily practices. Similarly, an initial survey of the tasks of representing, legislating, and monitoring that are duties of all members of parliament indicates that the majority of evangelicals who walk in the corridors of power were improvising politicians who were not sufficiently prepared to exercise a public function and who did not have a basic knowledge of how power relations are woven in the complex world of politics. The data accumulated during all of these years also indicates that pastors and evangelical leaders were not free to make instrumental use of their spiritual authority in order to politically orient local church members in electoral situations regarding the temptation to enter the public life to become part of the circles of power, the seduction of individual leadership, and the extemporized political vocations and authoritarian practices. A critical analysis of the evangelical members of congress and of the political attitudes of pastors and evangelical leaders in electoral processes during the so-called "Peru of Fujimori" (1990–2000) demonstrates thus.[1]

The reality described, panoramically, establishes the need to continue examining the biblical foundations of mission entrusted to the church and to continue reflecting theologically both on the church-world relationship and on various topics pertaining to public ethics. This continued reflection is needed for two reasons. First, it is necessary because many so-called "evangelical politicians" have followed the traditional way of doing politics. In fact, like the professional politicians or the old political class, evangelicals who entered into the realm of public affairs in recent years have also made use of political patronage, nepotism, opportunism, and manipulation of the means of social communication with those of evangelical background. All of this was done with the purpose of acceding to certain levels of power and with the clear intention of remaining in these public spaces arguing that they represent the legitimate interests of evangelical churches and that they were their official spokespersons on political issues. Second, continued examination is important because within certain evangelical circles of distinct theological backgrounds, it is still believed that pastoral authority is related to an uncritical submission of the members of various evangelical congregations to the final word of the "servants" of God, both on topics concerning doctrine and ecclesiastical discipline and on social themes and political subjects. Even

---

1. I have registered these facts and specific data pertaining to this study in a document not yet published entitled, *La Seducción del Poder: Evangélicos y Política en el "Perú de Fujimori"* [The Seduction of Power: Evangelicals and Politics in "Fujimori's Peru"]. In this document, I explain that the public presence of evangelical women in the Survival Organizations and the presence of evangelical peasants in the Committees of Self-Defense, better known as the Peasant Patrols, was radically distinct from that of the evangelical parliament members tied to Fujimori's government.

a significant number of the pastors and leaders of evangelical churches presuppose that their authority as spiritual guides has as its natural counterpart the submissive obedience of church members to their political opinion and particular electoral orientation.

What does the Bible say about these critical subjects? Is it possible to articulate a theology of political action, or in every case to outline guiding principles for Christian testimony in the public sphere? Particularly, what are the biblical foundations upon which the handling of power and the exercise of delegated authority should be based? Biblical texts like Luke 22:24–27 (cf. Matt 20:20–28; Mark 10:35–45) are key in responding to these questions. There fundamental criteria for a Christian presence in the realm of politics and substantive principles for examining the conduct of individual and collective actors in this realm of human life are outlined.

THE LUCAN TESTIMONY

The theme of power is one of the transversal axes of Luke's gospel.[2] The political dimension of this theme is sufficiently stressed throughout the third gospel.[3] A panoramic examination of the infancy accounts of Jesus of Nazareth recorded only by Luke amply illustrates this. The *Magnificat* or song of Mary (Luke 1:46–55), the *Benedictus* or song of Zechariah (Luke 1:67–79), and the *Nunc Dimittis* or song of the elderly Simeon (Luke 2:29–32) give account of this. So, for example, the undeniable political content of the *Magnificat* insinuates that for Mary messianic hope aims at a total transformation of social relations and a radical inversion of the pyramid of power. According to Carlos Escudero Freire, this song presents God as "existing within history, near, close, the companion, guide, and defender of the people. . . . The Lord is the God of Israel, of their experience and historic liberation, the God of the exodus, which

2. José Míguez Bonino defines power as "a set of social relations through which a group of individuals is able to direct and control a society" (Míguez Bonino, *Poder del Evangelio*, 24, my translation).

3. In Luke's gospel references to the themes of authority (*exousia*) and of power (*dunamis*) are more frequent than in the gospels of Matthew and Mark. The word *exousia* (*authority or power*) signifies legitimate, real, or full power to act, control, use, or make use of someone or something. This word appears 102 times in the New Testament and is used sixteen times in Luke, while it is used on ten occasions in Matthew and Mark. The word *dunamis* (power, capacity, force, or miracles) signifies physical power or ability to achieve something. Luke uses this word on fifteen occasions, Matthew thirteen times, and Mark has eleven references to it.

becomes the paradigm for other historic liberations."[4] And the content of the words of the elder Simeon (Luke 2:25) and of the prophetess Anna (Luke 2:38) indicate that for both the presence of the Messiah on the stage of history was connected to the liberation of his people. As John Howard Yoder suggests: "Now whatever be the 'actual historical shape' of the events lying behind the story, we can be assured that, in the atmosphere of heightened apocalyptic sensitivity into which Jesus came, it was at least *possible* if not *normal* for those who were 'waiting for the consolation of Israel' to see in these miraculous deliverances of the Old Testament story a paradigm of the way God would save his people now."[5]

In his gospel Luke does not avoid, then, the theme of politics or the theme of power.[6] Rather, he presents Jesus as the Messiah promised by the prophets of the Old Testament, whose inaugural discourse or programmatic platform expounded in the synagogue of Nazareth constitutes a clear indicator both of the content and of the reach of his liberating mission (Luke 4:16–30). According to the Lucan testimony, the liberating mission of Jesus of Nazareth aimed to reverse the destiny of the poor and of the sectors condemned to social ostracism such as women, tax collectors, Samaritans, and lepers. For Saint Luke, Jesus' proclamation regarding the kingdom of God had unquestionable political connotations and dimensions. The entire gospel testifies to this. However, exclusively Lucan passages like Luke 13:32, in which Jesus calls Herod Antipas, the worldly authority of the time, "that fox," are especially remarkable in capturing the theological texture of the third gospel regarding the theme of political power. The same can be said about the political character of the preaching of John the Baptist (Luke 3:1–18), a prophet who also publicly criticized Herod Antipas. Also, it should not be forgotten that only Luke situates the history of Jesus of Nazareth in its specific historical context, mentioning by name the worldly authorities like the Roman emperors Caesar Augustus (Luke 2:1) and Tiberius Caesar (Luke 3:1), Quirinius the governor of Syria (Luke 2:2), the Roman governor of Judea Pontius

4. Escudero Freire, *Devolver el Evangelio*, 200–201.

5. Yoder, *Politics of Jesus*, 87.

6. From a biblical perspective, God has the only legitimate and full authority, as only he has authority in himself. In this sense, all human authority is delegated or conferred, and worldly rulers will have to answer to God for how they use their respective positions or spaces of power.

Pilate (Luke 3:1), and Herod the tetrarch of Galilee (Luke 3:19). The same is done in Acts, as the events are located in their precise historical context.

Particularly in Luke 22:1–71, the theme of political power is especially detailed in relation to the contrast between the values of the kingdom of God and the values that support the kingdoms of this world, orchestrated by the "power [*exousia*] of darkness" (Luke 22:53). All of chapter 22 in Luke's gospel records what could be designated as the hour of the power of darkness. There the plot to kill Jesus is recorded, in which one of his disciples, Judas Iscariot, participates actively (Luke 22:1–6), the institution of the Lord's Supper (Luke 22:7–23), the prediction of Peter's denial (Luke 22:31–34), Jesus' prayer in Gethsemane (Luke 22:39–46), the arrest of Jesus (Luke 22:47–53), Peter's denials (Luke 22:54–62), and their trial of Jesus (Luke 22:63–71). It is also interesting to note that in this chapter several references are made to the word "sword" (Luke 22:36, 38, 49, 52), an instrument or weapon of war, whose political significance does not require explanation, especially if it is associated with the existence of groups resistant to the Roman presence in Palestine, such as revolutionaries like the Zealots or the *sicarii* (assassins).

Precisely with these things as a backdrop is placed the account of the discussion of Jesus' disciples in the upper room regarding who of them would be the most important or the greatest.[7] Why? What did Luke intend to communicate to his readers? One significant fact can help us to understand the particular intention of the author of the third gospel. A declaration Jesus made when he was arrested by the Jewish authorities in Gethsemane, recorded only by Luke in his gospel, is especially worthy of attention. According to Luke, the words uttered by Jesus on this occasion were, "But this is your hour, and the power of darkness!" (Luke 22:53). The idea seems to be that even the discussion of Jesus' disciples, regarding ranks or places of preeminence in the kingdom of God, formed part of Satan's plan of destruction that had already previously overtaken Judas Iscariot (Luke 22:3–4) and now was attempting to attract the attention of the other disciples so that they might be seduced by the world's logic or by the predominant cultural patterns relating to the subject of political

7. In the gospels of Matthew and of Mark, the account of the disciples' discussion has as an immediate backdrop events distinct from those narrated in Luke's gospel. Further on, specifically in Matt 26:1–75 and Mark 4:1–72, the events mentioned by Luke in his gospel are recorded (Luke 22:1–71). In addition, Luke places the account of the disciples' discussion during the institution of the Lord's Supper in the upper room.

power. Indeed, it seems that it was so. When the popular idea of the time of access to political power under the commonly accepted leadership model as the selfish pursuit of personal and family benefits was introduced into the circle of disciples, they were acting like worldly characters who governed the pagan nations of the time.

Does this mean that politics is in essence a merely worldly activity? Is the realm of politics entirely under the dominion of Satan and his human instruments? What then is the role of members of the community of disciples as citizens? How should they act within the *polis* (city) of which they form a part? Luke 22:24–27, as I have already pointed out, delineates key principles that respond to all of these questions. What does the biblical text say? The Lucan version of this incident, the disciples' discussion in the upper room regarding places of preeminence in the kingdom of God, states the following:

> A dispute also arose among them as to which one of them was to be regarded as the greatest. But he said to them, "The kings of the Gentiles lord it over them; and those in authority over them are called benefactors. But not so with you; rather the greatest among you must become like the youngest, and the leader like one who serves. For who is greater, the one who is at the table or the one who serves? Is it not the one at the table? But I am among you as one who serves.

Three central subjects relating to the theme of political power can be drawn from this biblical text. Each one of them encloses lessons that are interwoven within themselves and that are particularly pertinent for this time in which a growing percentage of pastors and evangelical leaders of distinct theological backgrounds affirm having been called by God to enter into the realm of politics. What should be considered as inescapable biblical criteria?

HUMAN ASPIRATIONS

One of the themes present in Luke 22:24–27 is that of human aspirations pertaining especially to the matter of power. There is related the discussion that the disciples of Jesus of Nazareth had about the places of preeminence that they would have in the immanent (according to them) establishment of the kingdom of God. The biblical text indicates the following regarding this key moment: "A dispute also arose among them as to which one of them was to be regarded as the greatest" (Luke 22:24). In light of the information that we have about the historical context, we can say that the discussion of the disciples of Jesus of Nazareth was associated with their theological presuppositions and politics characteristic of the Jewish cultural context of the time. Like many of their contemporaries, Jesus' disciples believed that the kingdom of God promised by the prophets of the Old Testament would be exclusively restricted to a defined geographical space (Israel) and would have a concrete political dimension (liberation from the situation of oppression that the Jewish people found themselves in at the moment). This is what is derived, for example, from a reading and analysis of biblical texts like Matt 20:20–28, Mark 10:35–45, and Acts 1:6, in which reference is made to topics like status and the geographical restoration of the kingdom of Israel. More specifically, biblical texts like the following amply illustrate the central point of the discussion that the disciples had in the upper room:

> Then the mother of the sons of Zebedee came to him with her sons, and kneeling before him, she asked a favor of him. And he said to her, "What do you want?" She said to him, "Declare that these two sons of mine will sit, one at your right hand and one at your left, in your kingdom" (Matt 20:20–21).
>
> James and John, the sons of Zebedee, came forward to him and said to him, "Teacher, we want you to do for us whatever we ask of you." And he said to them, "What is it you want me to do for you?" And they said to him, "Grant us to sit, one at your right hand and one at your left, in your glory" (Mark 10:35–37).
>
> So when they had come together, they asked him, "Lord, is this the time when you will restore the kingdom to Israel?" (Acts 1:6).

Why is all of this information about popular ideas that existed regarding the advent of promised Messiah important? Because this precise cultural and theological context characteristic of the Jewish political-religious world of the first century allows us to better understand both the motivations and the individual and familial aims that were behind the dispute or discussion of Jesus' disciples regarding status and capacity to exercise dominion over others. The accounts of Matthew, Mark, and Luke indicate that the establishment of the kingdom of God was near, and for that reason, they sought to secure the foremost places or the places of preeminence in the messianic kingdom. As Luke states in his gospel,

"He was near Jerusalem, and . . . they supposed that the kingdom of God [*basileia tou theou*] was to appear immediately" (Luke 19:11). Even more, a comparative analysis of Luke 22:24, Matt 20:24, and Mark 10:41 shows that the discussion about the subject of power permeated the mentality of all of the disciples, and not only the sons of Zebedee and their mother.[8] None of them were free from ambition for power as they all were thinking in the same terms. And, according to the Lucan testimony, it was actually not the first occasion in which Jesus' disciples discussed this subject among themselves, as Luke 9:46–48 indicates. There it states that, "An argument arose among them as to which one of them was the greatest" (Luke 9:46). According to the accounts of the synoptic gospels, the search for places of privilege, preeminence, status, and power, which expressed itself clearly in the collective discussion about who among them would be the most important or the greatest, also manifested itself in such human passions as argument (Luke 22:24) and anger (Matt 20:24; Mark 10:41). In other words, within the community of disciples, the fight to obtain the positions of preeminence or the places of prominence expressed itself in selfish and worldly human actions and undoubtedly broke and hurt the relationships, companionship, and solidarity that should have existed among the followers of the Teacher from Galilee.

Luke points out that "a dispute also arose among them" (Luke 22:24), while Matthew and Mark stress that after the request of the mother of the sons of Zebedee, the disciples "were angry with the two brothers" (Matt 20:24), or "began to be angry with James and John" (Mark 10:41). These biblical texts indicate that the discussion of Jesus' disciples was not solely limited to the political-religious ambitions of John and his brother James. This was not the case, as according to the biblical text, the "thirst for power" and the search for places of preeminence marked the life project of all of the members of the community of disciples. The fact that there was a dispute or a quarrel regarding who among them would be the greatest reveals both the disciples' mood and the theological climate in which their discussion was situated—it was neither one of solidarity nor

8. According to Matthew's gospel, it was the mother of the sons of Zebedee who asked Jesus for her sons John and James to sit in the places of preeminence in his kingdom (Matt 20:20–21). Using as a foundation the information reported in Mark 15:40, Mark 16:1, Matt 27:56, and John 19:25, biblical texts that mention information about the women who were present at the crucifixion and who went on Sunday morning to the place where Jesus had been buried, it is presumed that Salome was the name of the mother of the sons of Zebedee.

of comradeship. It was the exact opposite, especially because the discussion or dispute between the disciples turned to critical themes like the positions of privilege that they would have in the earthly kingdom that, according to their theological perspective, Jesus would soon inaugurate. The discussion, then, pertains to the capacity for political dominion and for the exercise of power that those who would sit at the right and the left of the throne would have, as those places customarily represented positions of preeminence or of status in the ancient world.[9] The discussion of the disciples of Jesus of Nazareth was, then, a discussion whose political slant is undeniable. But was it only a problem that affected the disciples of that time?

Human nature marked by selfishness that expresses itself through things like the desire for power and the fight to obtain positions of preeminence, within and outside of religious communities, has not changed. The experience of the disciples of Jesus of Nazareth continues to be the experience of human beings—among them evangelicals—of the contemporary global village. The relevance of the previous finding lies in its practical implications for Christian testimony in the world. Thus, for example, it can be pointed out that actions like fighting to obtain positions of prestige and tending to instrumentally use political or religious power form part of social reality and affect to a greater or lesser degree human relations in the public sphere and the relations of brotherhood within evangelical communities. These findings do not deny, of course, the legitimacy of aspiring to positions of preeminence in denominational structures or of exercising public responsibilities in the political realm or in organizations of civil society. However, the disciples of Jesus of Nazareth must be sufficiently conscious that the basic problem lies in individual motivations and in collective motivations, principally in the *why*, the motivation of one to aspire to reach a determined position of power within a political or religious structure, and in the *how*, the way, vehicle, or means of finally arriving in that position of power in the public sphere or in religious communities.

The disciples of Jesus of Nazareth are called—this is the demand of the gospel and the concrete way of realizing their identity as salt of the

---

9. The places of preeminence in the royal courts, in battles, and in public ceremonies were located to the right and to the left of the monarch's throne or the place occupied by the visible leader of the people. See, for example, biblical texts like Exod 17:12, 2 Sam 16:6, 1 Kgs 22:19, and Neh 8:4.

earth and light of the world—to have both holy motivations for obtaining positions of power and holy conduct in the exercise of conferred authority, whether within ecclesiastical structures or within a public function. This implies that endemic human passions, like the ambition for power or the fight over places of preeminence, need to be redeemed so that the *love of power* that is present not only in the public sphere, but also within different Christian denominations, might be replaced completely by the *power of love*. For the disciples of Jesus of Nazareth, it must be sufficiently clear that spurious motivations like the thirst for power or selfish ambitions and all of the worldly ways of accessing power, like the manipulation of collective wills and the use of spiritual authority for electoral ends, are not precisely evangelical virtues, but rather a negation of the Christian identity and ways of adapting to the predominant methods of power. The experience of all of these years indicates that Christians, as human beings of flesh and bone immersed in concrete political opportunities, have not always acted in conformity to the ethic of the kingdom of God, whether in the public life or in the exercise of spiritual authority conferred by the Lord.

THE PRACTICE OF POWER IN THE WORLD

According to the Lucan account, Jesus had been observant of the dispute between his disciples regarding the places of preeminence in the kingdom. The phrase "but he said to them" is sufficiently indicative of this point. Even more, Jesus' words recorded in Luke 22:25 show that in his remarks he highlights a political interpretation or reading of the historical context of the time. Jesus' words indicate that he has no illusions about the power structures or about the use of violence in the kingdoms of this world. This is so, because in Luke 22:25 and the parallel passages of Matt 20:25 and Mark 10:42, it is stressed that Jesus understood the way pagan rulers—perhaps he was thinking of Herod Antipas or the Roman emperor—handled, controlled, and articulated power relations in the nations under their order or their lordship.[10] According to Luke, these were the words of Jesus on this occasion: "The kings of the Gentiles lord it over them; and those in authority over them are called benefactors" (Luke

---

10. According to José Míguez Bonino, "In Mark 10:35–45 and its parallels in Matthew and Luke, our Lord defines the nature of his sovereignty in contradistinction to the image of the 'kings' or 'rulers of non-Jewish peoples.' One can easily think of the figure of the Roman emperor (the Caesar)" (*Poder del Evangelio*, 29, my translation).

22:25). The key idea in this critical examination of Jesus, particularly the saying about the abuse of power by those who have command in this world, is that authoritarian personalities formed part of the political reality of his time. Kings governed with tyranny and oppressed their subjects. In this specific historical context, all of the power was concentrated in the *basiléus* (kings), persons who were absolute rulers of the *éthnos* (nations) that they controlled tightly. It seems that Jesus' words were—especially in light of the version in Mark's gospel—a direct critique of the way Herod the Tetrarch, also known as Herod Antipas, the autocrat or territorial lord in this historical context, exercised political power. This especially seems to be the case because the meaning of Jesus' words "those whom they recognize as their rulers" (Mark 10:42), suggests a certain irony in his critique of the autocrat of the time, especially since the term *dokousin* ("those whom they recognize") can be more precisely translated as "'so-called' or 'those who are reputed to be' or 'are supposed to be.'"[11] There is no doubt then that in these words of Jesus there is an underlying critical note regarding the conduct of worldly rulers. This is further reaffirmed if we consider the way the NIV translates the final phrase of Luke 22:25: "call themselves Benefactors." This indicates that autocrats and tyrants who exercise power in a despotic way do not recognize the authoritarian character of their regime; on the contrary, they presume to be kindhearted rulers and generous territorial lords who give themselves the title of benefactors or those who benefit the people.

Authoritarian practices are nothing new in light of past history; they are not a contemporary development or a passing fashion in the complex world of politics. The presence of autocrats is one of the distinct features of all regimes in which the exercise of political power is concentrated in an individual or group of individuals who lord it over the social web and the political community, using the structure of the State to remain in power. More than a coincidence or a circumstantial political accident, authoritarian political personalities and projects have been constant in the history of peoples. This explains why, according to the author of the third gospel, Jesus himself pointed out that in relations of authority and in the exercise of power, those who have authority or the rulers are called or call themselves benefactors (Luke 22:25).[12] Put in another way, this

11. Hendriksen, *Mark*, 413.

12. This is not strange, as in the Greek cultural world, they were accustomed to giving the honorable title of benefactor of the people to gods, to kings, and to other important

biblical text indicates that those who *exousiazō* (have authority) within an absolutist political project legitimate and validate their presence in those places of preeminence by making concessions or performing favors for the courtiers or for the elite who support them and for the people who back their rule, with the end of securing the concentration of all of the power and authority in their hands.[13] These earthly lords, ephemeral and transitory, love it when their subjects recognize the "kindnesses" of their government or of the regime they represent, calling them *euergetēs* (benefactors), or referring to themselves in this way. This has been the case, it still continues occurring, and certainly it will continue to form part of the way earthly authorities make their subjects feel all of the weight of the political power that they have. Does not the same occur in our time?

This is verified in the history of nations. Indeed, the presence of autocrats and their permanence in the center of power for long periods leans on both a network of courtiers who support and sustain their authoritarian project in this way and on articulation of a set of mechanisms whose end is to secure the regime's operation for an extremely prolonged period. But while they do this, designing refined mechanisms of social control and political repression, the autocrats in turn expect that those who are under their authority believe that their greatest concern is the interests for whom, according to their particular point of view, they keep watch over at all times. These earthly tyrants who oppress their subjects have been called, as Jesus pointed out in this instance, benefactors of the people. It is also pleasing to them for the people to call them protectors or liberators. Have not the autocrats and the dictators of our time done the same?

THE ETHIC OF THE KINGDOM OF GOD

An examination of Luke 22:26–27 allows us to establish that for Jesus, there are two fundamental, interconnected features that should clearly distinguish the exercise of power within the community of disciples from

---

persons of the time. Even more, kings in the ancient world were accustomed to calling themselves *euergetēs* or benefactors. Regarding this, one fact relevant to our study is that of all the New Testament documents, only Luke's gospel uses this word.

13. The word *exousiazō*, used in Luke 22:25, appears only four times in the New Testament (it is also used in 1 Cor 6:12 and 1 Cor 7:4) and is translated as: to have authority, to let dominate, or to have power. The other word translated as authority is *exousía*, which is used on 102 occasions in the New Testament and is translated as authority, power, jurisdiction, liberty, or justice.

the exercise of power in the world: motivations and concrete practice. The interpretive key of Luke 22:26–27, from my point of view, is found in the following words uttered by Jesus when he became aware of the central problem that was behind the quarrel or heated discussion of the disciples regarding rank and status in the kingdom of God: "But not so with you; rather the greatest among you must become like the youngest, and the leader like one who serves" (Luke 22:26). Jesus' words "but not so with you" indicate that the disciples, as citizens of the kingdom of God, had to forget about rank, preeminence, and prominence. Jesus thus prepares them for both the seduction and the danger of power. He desires for the community of disciples to be a counterculture with respect to the predominant reality and an alternative community distinct from the political formations of the world. Undoubtedly, Jesus expected that his disciples be totally different from other persons, both in the motivations that they should have to reach places of preeminence or positions of privilege, and in the exercise of delegated or conferred authority. In order to be different from others, of course, an epistemological transformation and a substantial change in daily conduct are needed. These things give account of a radical *metanoia* or a genuine conversion. This is so because in the community of disciples the pyramid of power is inverted, as greatness, whose foundation is sacrificial love expressed in unselfish service to one's neighbor, consists of giving oneself so that others might enjoy the fullness of life that the gospel offers. Consequently, the values of the surrounding society and the traditional ways of reaching places of preeminence in the world do not apply in the community of disciples, where human relations have radically distinct tones. Therefore, access to the places of privilege has as the point of departure the demand to become a servant of others following the example of their Lord and Teacher. In the words of Jesus recorded by Mark in his gospel, "And whoever wishes to be first among you must be slave of all. For the Son of Man came not to be served but to serve, and to give his life a ransom for many" (Mark 10:44–45).

Jesus did not call his disciples for them to be *kurioi* (lords), but *diakonoi* (ministers or servants) and *douloi* (servants), setting himself as the paradigm or concrete model. This is unquestionably expressed in the following words of Jesus recorded by Luke in his gospel: "But I am among you as one who serves [*diakoneō*]" (Luke 22:27).[14] In light of this, Jesus is

14. In the parallel biblical text of Mark 10:43–44, the words *diákonos* (10:43) and *doulos* (10:44) are practically used as synonyms. Both words, if the context is kept in

the *diakonos* par excellence. He rejects every human means of fighting for status and demands that his disciples in their various social relations—and when they should be in a position to exercise power on the distinct levels of human life—act as he acted, and not like the earthly authorities whose scale of values is radically different from the principles of the reign of God.[15] In the ancient world, the great personages of the time sat at tables so that persons of a lower social status, the *doulos* and *diakonos*, served them or attended to them. The same occurs in our time, as the positions of status and power of each person can be noted by the places that the public personages occupy in ceremonies and in official receptions. But in the reign of God, greatness is neither defined by status nor by the capacity for domination that an individual has, but by the capacity for sacrificial service to others and by the disposition to give one's life out of love for neighbor. "Authority legitimates itself in service"[16] and power makes sense only as service.[17] Jesus, by his attitude and by his words, stresses the need for a radical transformation of society into a culture without ranks or privileges. In this sense, John Howard Yoder is right when he expresses that Jesus reprimands his disciples "for having misunderstood the character of that new social order which he does intend to set up. The novelty of its character is not that it is not social, or not visible, but that it is marked by an alternative to accepted patterns of leadership. The alternative to how the kings of the earth rule is not 'spirituality' but servanthood."[18]

The kingdom of God is a kingdom that has only one King. In this kingdom, one does not get accustomed to naming heirs or successors to the King as in human kingdoms, for all of the members of the kingdom share the same identity as disciples who serve a single Lord and recognize a sole Teacher, whose example of service to the point of sacrifice constitutes the norm and the paradigm of greatness. Is this not a call to act at

---

mind, can be translated as minister or as servant. Technically, the word *diakonos* is related to the task of serving at the table of the employer or master, while the word *doulos* means slave and reflects a condition of servanthood.

15. The word *diakoneō* appears thirty-six times in the New Testament, mostly in the gospels and in several of the Pauline epistles. It can be translated as: to serve, to minister, to send, to administrate, to exercise deaconship, or to help. The related nouns are *diakonos* (servant) and *diakonia* (service).

16. Míguez Bonino, *Poder del Evangelio*, 29, my translation.

17. Ibid., 26–29.

18. Yoder, *Politics of Jesus*, 46.

all times like a counterculture rather than adapting to the predominant mentality or letting oneself get absorbed by the "spirit" of the world?

The ethic of the kingdom of God undoubtedly has a foundation and a horizon completely different from the values that shape and control power relations in social spaces distinct from the community of Jesus' disciples. One hopes that in the community of Jesus' disciples, the desire for power and authoritarian practices so common in the surrounding world will be replaced by the evangelical motivation of love for neighbor and selfless service to all human beings, as for the disciples of the Teacher from Galilee the model is Jesus of Nazareth and the utopian horizon is the kingdom of God. This explains why subordinate motivation and all authoritarian practice, all unhealthy search for the foremost positions, all theological pride and political ethnocentrism constitute a negation of the Christian identity of all those who, presenting themselves as citizens of the kingdom of God, have not yet parted from these mundane practices. Jesus calls us to be different. Regarding this, his words, "But not so with you," outline the route that all of his disciples must travel. They should be different from others both in motivations and in concrete practice.

PASTORAL GUIDELINES FOR TODAY

What are the lessons for us? What can we learn about human aspirations, the way authority is used in power structures, and the inversion of values that the kingdom of God demands? Is it possible to articulate pastoral guidelines upon which political practice and the exercise of authority rest? This does not mean developing an instruction manual or an undisputable pastoral prescription. It is possible, however, to put together principles that contribute to thinking and acting biblically in a terrain where evangelical presence has not necessarily been distinct from that of other collective actors or social characters. In order to walk through the corridors of power and in order to act in the realm of politics neither religious discourse nor good intentions are sufficient. It is necessary to know what is done in this realm and how agreements and consensuses are achieved between different actors present in the political community. What should be taken into account?

First, it is important to be sufficiently conscious that the fight to accede places of preeminence and the ambition for power form part of human nature and have shaped the history of all nations. Even the disciples of Jesus of Nazareth were not "vaccinated" against these very real and contemporary human passions. The same can also be observed when one examines the history of the Christian church and the daily experience of many present-day evangelical communities in distinct historical contexts. Specifically, one of the basic problems within the relations of authority and subordination lies in the motivations that catalyze or propel human actions, as they frequently translate into an instrumental use of authority and power for the obtainment of personal or collective benefits and advantages. And so selfish motivations that seek affirmation and the satisfaction of personal desires, as well as the desires of the group that supports certain leadership, are part of social reality and reveal the human face of the church and the human condition of political actors. The problem is exacerbated when we realize that we evangelicals are not as holy as we aim to be and that worldliness has smuggled its way into the life of evangelical churches. In other words, the passions and motivations of the flesh are reflected in the use that we make of delegated authority and of the power that we have, when it seduces us, molds our personal and collective conduct, and feeds our ambition and pride.

Second, the authoritarian practice or lordship of rulers of the nations constitutes a fact of historical reality that marks the exercise of political power in the kingdoms of this world. It is nothing new to affirm that the history of nations gives account of this fact. So, from the power structures, autocrats weave or put together an ample network of social and political relations with the clear objective of consolidating their power and that of the elite who accompany them in their political venture. This concentration of power in the hands of an individual, and in the group that supports and validates the authoritarian character of the government, demands, on one hand, a hardening of the regime's or the State's coercive role, or on the other hand, a perfecting of repressive methods. This is the case, because in order to secure the regime's validity, every sign or mark of resistance must be silenced or simply demolished, as autocrats do not tolerate the existence of opponents to their authoritarian project. History teaches that one of the "strategies" used by authoritarian regimes to remain in power is the offering of political favors, making use of the mechanisms of pressuring the State or of the material needs of the poor, with the intention of promoting the popularity of the *basileus* so that they may be recognized as benefactors. The experience of all of these years precisely indicates that authoritarian governments need an unconditional nucleus of courtiers who validate the gears of the regime and help the autocrat, in turn, to remain in power for a prolonged period. To this end, particularly in the poor nations of the world, they make an instrumental use of social organizations, or, in any case, they break up the sources of political resistance and annul basic civil rights. That is, the entire structure of and institutions connected to the State are put into the service of the determined political regime, so that it may prolong its term and remain in power.

Third, an internalization of the values of the kingdom of God reflects itself clearly in a lifestyle based in selfless service to others. This implies that the social practice and political practice of the disciples of Jesus of Nazareth must at all times be profoundly permeated with and catalyzed by gospel values like truth, solidarity, transparency, and justice. This entails that holiness is more than a simple article of faith or a mere doctrinal principle; it must be a visible mark that differentiates the lifestyle of disciples when they exercise ecclesiastical or political power from the other ways of exercising authority and doing politics that exist in the mission environment. The duty of disciples consists of not letting the passions and values that characterize the social relations and the practice of power in the kingdoms of this world change their holy motivations or disfigure and annul their identity as citizens of the kingdom of God, whose ethical foundation is non-negotiable and whose lifestyle cannot and should not be turned into a mere article for consumption subject to the laws of the market. The concrete model of Jesus of Nazareth as the Servant King challenges us to a service of sacrificial love that transmits and shares new life. What does this mean? It means that all authoritarian personality and practice, all love for power, all eagerness or desire to lord over others, are clear denials of the values of the kingdom of God. Within the kingdom community, received authority legitimates itself in a concrete practice of service to one's neighbor. This practice should be constantly nourished by gospel values such as solidarity, justice, and the pursuit of the common good or comradeship.

In light of the analyzed biblical text, one understands that a substantial difference must exist between the way that power is understood and practiced in the kingdoms of this world and the way that the disciples of Jesus of Nazareth understand and exercise the delegated power that they have. In this difference of starting points and guiding principles, rather linked together, both motivations and social conduct that visibly expresses those motivations are fundamental. Selfish motivations aimed at the use of political or religious power for the benefit of an individual or of an elite group, such as an authoritarian practice that manifests itself in acts like the violation of the human rights of the most vulnerable social sectors, among others, are two of the marks that profile the way delegated authority is understood and how power is used in the kingdoms of this world. This should not be so, neither for disciples as citizens of a certain *polis* in which they must give testimony of the kingdom of God and his justice, nor as members of the kingdom community within which both motivation and values are absolutely distinct from the lifestyle of the world.

Finally, admitting that evangelicals are not "vaccinated" against the temptation of love for power and other endemic human problems like corruption and nepotism, one should take into account that service based in love, rather than a search for personal or collective profit, must be the defining characteristic of the presence of the community of disciples as the salt of the earth and the light of the world. This implies that the disciples of Jesus of Nazareth must understand that in a political vocation one must be as holy as in any other vocation based on a clear and unmistakable call from the Lord of life and of history. It should not be forgotten that the disciples of Jesus of Nazareth must fight against the contemporary temptation to convert different evangelical churches into a kind of "chaplains" of the government, turning them into "official spokespersons" of a particular regime or into religious instruments of the State. The altar should never be subordinated to the interests of the throne.[19] In addition, it will always be necessary to remember the model of life is Jesus of Nazareth, the *diakonos* par excellence, and that our utopian horizon is the kingdom of God and his justice. Regarding this, the words of John Calvin, the reformer from Geneva, seem pertinent for this time, in which, in electoral situations, improvising evangelical politicians emerge, limited in their understanding of political matters, and orphans of a programmatic platform whose aim should be the common good, rather than the pursuit of earthly benefits for evangelical churches. These were the words of John Calvin: "The Lord has not only testified that the function of magistrates has his approbation and acceptance, but has eminently commended it to us, by dignifying it with the most honourable titles."[20]

19. Rivera Pagán, *Fe y Cultura*, 67.

20. Calvin, *Institutes*, 773 (IV, XX, 4).

10

God's Special Love for the Poor and Marginalized

A Biblical Perspective

INTRODUCTION

One of the overarching thematic axes of Sacred Scripture is the special love that God has for the fragile of society.[1] Independent of particular hermeneutical approaches and theological conceptions, neither can the centrality and the transcendence of this key theme for the church's mission be avoided, nor can its liberating content and its catalyzing effect

---

1. The fragile—the poor and the marginalized—are the needy, the destitute, the insignificant, the scorned, the disposable, the ragged, the outcasts, the tattered, those who are on the periphery of society—in other words, the "nobodies" and the "nothings" according to the social, cultural, and economic criteria of predominant society. At present the fragile are considered as human trash, disposable articles, or disposable social sectors that the invisible hand of the market expectorates or expels as unnecessary leftovers of the system.

for Christian testimony be "spiritualized." God's special love for social sectors considered as insignificant and disposable by those who wield political and economic power, constitutes—from the lens of the kingdom of God—a non-negotiable hermeneutical key for the missionary reflection and practice of evangelical churches in all temporal settings in which they are situated to publicly proclaim their unbreakable faith in the crucified and resurrected Jesus of Nazareth. This is an inescapable theme for the common agenda of Christian churches, particularly in regard to its concrete consequences for integral mission.

THE PERSPECTIVE OF THE OLD TESTAMENT

The richness of the underlying content of the words that are used in the Old Testament to identify the poor and the excluded is provocative and challenging. It is provocative because it demands a rigorous examination of the theological presuppositions upon which our collective and challenging task is articulated, because it restates or redesigns the concrete missional practice of evangelical churches. In the Old Testament, the poor person is the *dal*, the weak one, the one who has been stripped of his or her possessions, the insignificant person who has been beaten and does not have enough strength to get up.[2] The poor person is also the *ébyôn*, the beggar who hopes for the help of another, who is humiliated by the lowest level of poverty and who needs to be liberated from this situation.[3] The poor person is likewise the *ani*, the bent-over person who is below an enormous weight and who does not possess all of his ability

---

2. *Dal* appears forty-eight times in the Old Testament, principally in Job, Proverbs, and in the Prophets (Gen 41:19; Exod 23:3; 30:15; Lev 14:21; 19:15; Judg 6:15; 1 Sam 2:8; 2 Sam 3:1; 13:4; Ruth 3:10; Pss 41:2; 72:13; 82:3, 4; 113:7; Prov 10:15; 14:31; 19:4, 17; 21:13; 22:9, 16, 22 [2]; 28:3, 8, 11, 15; 29:7, 14; Job 5:16; 20:10, 19; 31:16; 34:19, 28; Isa 10:2; 11:4; 14:30; 25:4; 26:6; Jer 5:4; 39:10; Amos 2:7; 4:1; 5:11; 8:6; Zeph 3:12).

3. *Ébyôn* is used sixty-one times in the Old Testament, especially in Psalms and in the Prophets (Exod 23:6, 11; Deut 15:4, 7 [2], 9, 11 [2]; 24:14; 1 Sam 2:8; Esth 9:22; Pss 9:18; 12:5; 35:10; 37:14; 40:17; 49:2; 69:33; 70:5; 72:12, 13 [2]; 74:21; 82:4; 86:1; 107:41; 109:16, 22, 31; 112:9; 113:7; 132:15; 140:12; Prov 14:31; 30:14; 31:9, 20; Job 5:15; 24:4, 14; 29:16; 30:25; 31:19; Isa 14:30; 25:4; 29:19; 32:7; 41:17; Jer 2:34; 5:28; 20:13; 22:16; Ezek 16:49; 18:18; 22:29; Amos 2:6; 4:1; 5:12; 8:4, 6).

and vigor, the humiliated one, the afflicted one, the miserable one.[4] The poor is also the *anaw* or the one who is humble before God.[5]

Widows, orphans, and foreigners are the poor and the excluded of the Old Testament. This triad, representative of the defenseless and vulnerable social sectors, from the Old Testament perspective is human beings of flesh and bone whose dignity is being trampled on with impunity by those who wield political, economic, and religious power. Many are the occasions and the circumstances in which God demonstrates a special concern for the condition of material orphanhood and of violence in which they find themselves and expresses his compassion for the destitute and the needy, exploited by the rich and the powerful (Exod 22:22; Deut 10:17–19; 24:19–22; 26:12, 13; Pss 68:5; 146:9; Isa 1:17; 10:2; Jer 7:6; 22:3; Ezek 22:7; Zech 7:10; Mal 3:5). God's special love for these social sectors explains why he presents himself as father (Ps 68:5) and defender (Ps 146:9; Prov 22:22–23) of the weak and of the defenseless. God "loses face" for them (Ps 68:5; Prov 23:10–11). To him "the helpless commit themselves" and he is "the helper of the orphan" (Ps 10:14). Or as Deuteronomy states:

> For the LORD your God is God of gods and Lord of lords, the great God, mighty and awesome, who is not partial and takes no bribe, who executes justice for the orphan and the widow, and who loves the strangers, providing them food and clothing. (Deut 10:17–18)

The affirmation, "God is no respecter of persons," explains why the Mosaic legislation had clear prescriptions for their care (Deut 24:19–22), and why the rich had the obligation to fight for the poor and the marginalized of the community (Deut 15:1–11). Books like Leviticus and Deuteronomy contain commandments and specific ordinances to protect the defenseless social sectors (Deut 5:14; 14:28–29; 23:20, 26:12; Lev 19:9–10; 23:22; 25:2–7; 25:35–37). Moreover, the ethical instructions of

---

4. *Ani* is the word most used, as it appears eighty times in the Old Testament, fundamentally in Psalms and in the Prophets (Exod 22:24; Lev 19:10; 23:22; Deut 15:11; 24:12, 14, 15; 2 Sam 22:28; Pss 9:12, 19; 10:2, 9 [2], 12; 12:6; 14:6; 18:28; 22:25; 25:16; 34:7; 35:10 [2]; 37:14; 40:18; 68:11; 69:30; 70:5; 72:2, 4, 12; 74:19, 21; 82:3; 86:5; 88:16; 102:1; 109:16, 22; 140:13; Prov 3:34; 14:21; 15:15; 16:19; 22:22; 30:14; 31:9, 20; Job 24:4, 9, 14; 29:12; 34:28; 36:6, 15; Isa 3:14, 15; 10:2, 30; 14:32; 26:6; 32:7; 41:17; 49:13; 51:21; 54:11; 58:7; 66:2; Jer 22:16; Ezek 16:49; 18:12, 17; 22:29; Amos 8:4; Hab 3:14; Zeph 3:12; Zech 7:10; 9:9; 11:7, 11).

5. Gutiérrez, *Theology of Liberation*, 165.

the Old Testament specify that God demands that righteousness and justice (*tsedaqah* and *misphat*) be carried out at all times, become a gesture and daily concrete practice in all human relations, as he is righteous and loves righteous deeds (Ps 11:7). In this sense, God strips hypocritical religiosity, denouncing that injustice, exploitation, the bankruptcy of what is right, the objectification of human beings, and oppression are individual and collective sins that contradict his purpose of righteousness and of the establishment of justice. These are the reasons why he proclaims judgment and punishment for those who have infringed upon his law, doing violence to the right of the poor and excluded, treating them as disposable things. In the words of Isaiah:

> Ah, you who make iniquitous decrees,
> who write oppressive statutes,
> to turn aside the needy from justice
> and to rob the poor of my people of their right,
> that widows may be your spoil,
> and that you may make the orphans your prey!
> What will you do on the day of punishment,
> in the calamity that will come from far away?
> To whom will you flee for help,
> and where will you leave your wealth[?] (Isa 10:1–3)

As in the case of Isaiah, it was the prophets who publicly denounced the situation of marginalization and oppression in which the defenseless social sectors found themselves, stating that the rich and the powerful of the time were the perpetrators of this situation of violence against the human dignity of the poor. Within this reality of violence and death, the prophets of the Old Testament demanded the practice of justice and of righteousness. Regarding this, Amos the prophet of Tekoa was quite explicit in his denunciation:

> Hear this, you that trample on the needy,
> and bring to ruin the poor of the land,
> saying, "When will the new moon be over
> so that we may sell grain;
> and the sabbath,
> so that we may offer wheat for sale?
> We will make the ephah small and the shekel great,
> and practice deceit with false balances,
> buying the poor for silver

and the needy for a pair of sandals,
and selling the sweepings of the wheat."

The LORD has sworn by the pride of Jacob:
Surely I will never forget any of their deeds. (Amos 8:4–7)

And the public denunciation of Micah of Moresheth was no less emphatic than that of Amos the prophet of Tekoa:

And I said:
Listen, you heads of Jacob
and rulers of the house of Israel!
Should you not know justice?—
you who hate the good and love the evil,
who tear the skin off my people,
and the flesh off their bones;
who eat the flesh of my people,
flay their skin off them,
break their bones in pieces,
and chop them up like meat in a kettle,
like flesh in a caldron.

Then they will cry to the LORD,
but he will not answer them;
he will hide his face from them at that time,
because they have acted wickedly. . . .

Hear this, you rulers of the house of Jacob
and chiefs of the house of Israel,
who abhor justice
and pervert all equity,
who build Zion with blood
and Jerusalem with wrong!
Its rulers give judgment for a bribe,
its priests teach for a price,
its prophets give oracles for money;
yet they lean upon the LORD and say,
"Surely the LORD is with us!
No harm shall come upon us."
Therefore because of you
Zion shall be plowed as a field;
Jerusalem shall become a heap of ruins,
and the mountain of the house a wooded height.
(Mic 3:1–4, 9–12)

The prophets' strong denunciation points out that actions such as the gradual abandonment of God's law were correlated with a crude situation of immorality and injustice that especially affected the poor, especially because the ruling class condemned them to social ostracism, treating them as disposable objects or as leftovers according to the words of Amos and Micah. Within this situation of oppression, presenting God as the protector of the weak and of the defenseless, the prophets denounced the greedy social conduct and hypocritical religion of the ruling class of the time. The prophet Zephaniah was extremely clear:

> Ah, soiled, defiled,
> oppressing city!
> It has listened to no voice;
> it has accepted no correction.
> It has not trusted in the LORD;
> it has not drawn near to its God.
>
> The officials within it
> are roaring lions;
> its judges are evening wolves
> that leave nothing until the morning.
> Its prophets are reckless,
> faithless persons;
> its priests have profaned what is sacred,
> they have done violence to the law.
> The LORD within it is righteous;
> he does no wrong.
> Every morning he renders his judgment,
> each dawn without fail;
> but the unjust knows no shame. (Zeph 3:1–5)

And Habakkuk's denunciation is in the same prophetic vein:

> "Alas for you who get evil gain for your house,
> setting your nest on high
> to be safe from the reach of harm!"
> You have devised shame for your house
> by cutting off many peoples;
> you have forfeited your life.
> The very stones will cry out from the wall,
> and the plaster will respond from the woodwork.
>
> "Alas for you who build a town by bloodshed,
> and found a city on iniquity!" (Hab 2:9–12)

In their public denunciation the prophets painted a heartbreaking picture of corruption, violence, exploitation and moral degradation, monopolizing of lands and of foods, injustice and bribery, breaking of the law and abusive economy, usury and objectification of the human being (Isa 3:14–15; 5:26–31; 22:14–17; Amos 2:6; 4:1; 5:11–12; Mic 3:1–12; 6:6–12). This was the concrete context of death and violence in which the poor and excluded like widows, orphans, and foreigners found themselves. But God did not abandon them. In the Old Testament he presents himself as their *goèl*, their liberator, their refuge, their vindicator, and their protector. In the Mosaic legislation and in the message of the prophets, it is clear that God is the one who liberates the defenseless and unprotected social sectors (orphans, widows, and foreigners) from the subhuman condition in which they find themselves (Ps 146:5–9). It is not, however, an aspect of God's character that is restricted to the cultural context of the Old Testament. Also in today's globalized world in which the poor and the excluded are treated as disposable things and have been confined to the dung heap of history and to the dump of social relations, God values and treats them as human beings created in his image, whose dignity cannot be reduced or trampled, whether for reasons of the State or for demands of political economies. God has not quit being the *goèl* of the defenseless and the underprivileged.

Orphans, widows, and foreigners, the trilogy representing the poor and the excluded, are objects of God's special love and active subjects within his purpose of reconstructing all human relations. God dignifies the poor and the excluded, recognizes their position as human beings, and demands that his people do the same. Consequently, according to the scope of the Old Testament, the material poor and the insignificant of history have a preferential place in God's saving purpose. However, one cannot ignore that two meanings of poverty—material and spiritual—exist, which taken as a whole compose the backbone of the Old Testament perspective. According to a specialist on this topic:

> The O.T. had two terms for designating the poor: the poor man is, in the first place, the slave of men, one whom necessity places in a subordinate position, or who is obliged to beg (Deut. 24:14–15; Ps. 22:69); then, in the second place, he is one who, in relation to God, finds himself in a state of dependence, who obeys God as a slave obeys his master (Ps. 25:9; 34:2–3), who is responsive to his will (Ps. 25:15).

... In Scripture, therefore, we find two correlative senses of
poverty: material poverty and spiritual poverty, of which the latter ought to be the consequence of the former.[6]

Thus, on one hand, there are the material poor who do not have the
economic goods necessary to live decently. On the other hand, there are
the poor in spirit or the humble before God. In light of what has been
pointed out by Péry, it is clear that the expression "poor" went on gradu-
ally acquiring a meaning no longer solely in the material sense, but it also
obtained a spiritual dimension, practically equating poor as a synonym
of righteous, as is outlined in Ps 14:5–6. On one hand, there is material
poverty, a situation of exploitation, marginalization, and violence. On the
other hand, there is spiritual poverty, a state of openness, willingness, and
acceptance of the will of God. These are the two great meanings of poverty that weave the theological horizon of the Old Testament. However,
it should be clarified that concrete facts like the grim reality of material
poverty and the existence of poor persons such as widows and orphans
can neither be ignored nor spiritualized. This is demonstrated both by
the undeniable social concern underlying the Mosaic Law and by the emphatic protest of the prophets. The same can be said of the perspective of
the New Testament in which, although the two meanings of poverty (material and spiritual) are present as in the Old Testament, it is clear that the
poor in the economic sense of the term also exist and are human beings
of flesh and bone who live in objective conditions of exploitation, oppression, and material misery. In this sense, one cannot ignore, and much less
spiritualize, the structural causes that explain the subhuman condition in
which they find themselves prostrated, contrary to the purpose of God.

THE PERSPECTIVE OF THE NEW TESTAMENT

In the New Testament, the word most frequently used to designate a poor
person is *ptōchos*, the indigent and bent-over, "One who does not have
what is necessary to subsist, the wretched one driven into begging."[7] But
other words are also used to identify the poor, such as *penichros* (very

6. Péry, "Poor," 327.

7. Gutiérrez, *Theology of Liberation*, 165. The word *ptōchos* is used thirty-four times
in the New Testament, mostly in the gospels (Matt 5:3; 11:5; 19:21; 26:9, 11; Mark 10:21;
12:42, 43; 14:5, 7; Luke 4:18; 6:20; 7:22; 14:13, 21; 16:20, 22; 18:22; 19:8; 21:3; John 12:5,
6, 8; 13:29; Rom 15:26; 2 Cor 6:10; Gal 2:10; 4:9; Jas 2:2, 3, 5, 6; Rev 3:17; 13:16).

poor, wretched, needy), *hystereō* (poor), and *penēs* (poor or needy).[8] In reference to poverty, the words *ptōcheia* (2 Cor 8:2, 9; Rev 2:9) and *hysterēma* are used, two terms that portray the idea of absence, scarcity, necessity, and deficiency (Luke 21:4; 1 Cor 16:17; 2 Cor 8:14; 9:12; 11:9; Phil 2:30; Col 1:24; 1 Thess 3:10). The word *hysterēsis* is also used, which signifies indigence and need (Mark 12:44; Phil 4:11). Of all of these words, *ptōchos* is closest to the heart of what it means to be poor in the New Testament. The biblical references and corresponding support indicate thus, especially the testimony of the gospels, which describe the way Jesus of Nazareth related with the poor, treating them and valuing them as human beings created in the image of God.

The synoptic gospels, particularly the Lucan testimony, underline that during his traveling ministry through towns and villages, Jesus of Nazareth constantly related with the poor and excluded, the weak and the insignificant, the scorned and the less important, those who were on the periphery of society. Thus, social sectors like publicans (Matt 9:9–13; Luke 19:1–10), lepers (Matt 8:1–4; Luke 17:11–19), women (Matt 8:14–17; 9:18–26; 15:21–28; 26:6–13; 28:1–10; Mark 12:41–44; Luke 7:11–17), the sick (Matt 9:1–8; 12:9–14; 14:34–36; 20:29–34), children (Matt 19:13–15), and Samaritans (Luke 17:17–19; John 4:1–12) were at the center of his special love and his missionary concern. This radical practice of the carpenter from Nazareth (Matt 13:55; Mark 6:3) provoked in distinct moments and circumstances constant confrontations with religious leaders (Matt 9:1–8, 9–13; 12.9–14; Mark 2.1–12, 13–17; 3:1–3; Luke 5:27–32; 6:6–11; 13:10–17). The compassion of Jesus of Nazareth contrasted profoundly with the social short-sightedness and the spiritual blindness of the scribes and Pharisees, the representatives of the established religion of the time. In this sense, it can be argued that for Jesus of Nazareth, it was quite clear that "in light of the coming kingdom the differences between rich and poor are entirely against the will of God."[9] However, it was not only Jesus of Nazareth who showed a special concern for the indigent and the insignificant of society, as the apostolic church followed the same line of attention to the material needs of the poor and the excluded (Acts 2:41–47; 4:32–37; 6:1–7; 9:36–43; 11:29–30; 20:35). Paul recognized this in one of his first

---

8. *Penichros* is used only in Luke 21:2. *Hystereō* appears sixteen times in biblical texts like Matt 19:20; Mark 10:21; Luke 15:14; 22:35; 2 Cor 11:5, 9; Heb 11:37. *Pénes* is used only in 2 Cor 9:9.

9. Cullman, *Jesus and the Revolutionaries*, 25.

epistles when he tells of his encounter with the leaders of the Jerusalem church: "They asked only one thing, that we remember the poor [*ptōchos*], which was actually what I was eager to do" (Gal 2:10). René Padilla has similarly indicated, "Concern for the poor in the primitive church was a normal aspect of Christian discipleship. Translated into action, it made visible the life of the Kingdom inaugurated by Jesus Christ."[10]

The same practice and an identical concern can be perceived in the ministry of the apostle Paul, both in his teaching and its concrete impact on the life and the testimony of the communities of disciples located in distinct missionary contexts where the gospel of the kingdom of God was publicly proclaimed (Rom 15:25–29; 1 Cor 16:1–4; 2 Cor 8,9; Gal 2:10; Eph 4:28; Col 3:25; 1 Thess 4:11–12; 2 Thess 3:6–13; Phil 4:10–20; 1 Tim 5:10; Tit 3:14; Phlm 8–22). Likewise, the epistle of James clearly states what the evangelical attitude and practice should be in accordance with the purpose of God (Jas 2:1–26). Particularly, the prophetic vein of this New Testament document is quite explicit in passages like the following:

> Come now, you rich people, weep and wail for the miseries that are coming to you. Your riches have rotted, and your clothes are moth-eaten. Your gold and silver have rusted, and their rust will be evidence against you, and it will eat your flesh like fire. You have laid up treasure for the last days. Listen! The wages of the laborers who mowed your fields, which you kept back by fraud, cry out, and the cries of the harvesters have reached the ears of the Lord of hosts. You have lived on the earth in luxury and in pleasure; you have fattened your hearts in a day of slaughter. You have condemned and murdered the righteous one, who does not resist you. (Jas 5:1–6)

However, in the discussion regarding the New Testament perspective on poverty, one cannot evade the theme of the apparent contradiction that, according to certain authors, seems to exist in the meaning of poor used in the gospels of Matthew and Luke. This is a critical theme that has generated an ample debate among specialists. In this regard, the exegesis of key biblical texts from both gospels varies according to the theological orientation of the experts in New Testament studies. However, if one takes into account the theological scope of the Old Testament, the discussion regarding the New Testament perspective on poverty is also connected to the two meanings of poverty that weave together the entire message of

---

10. Padilla, *Mission between the Times*, 182.

Sacred Scripture: material poverty and spiritual poverty. René Padilla has acutely stated the heart of the discussion in the following terms: "It is true that in the Bible poverty cannot be reduced to the absence of material resources and that it can be taken for granted, without fear of error, that behind the use of the term 'poor' in the New Testament, there frequently lies an early Jewish tradition according to which 'poor' was almost a synonym for 'pious' or 'righteous.'"[11]

However, the same Padilla indicates that it is not possible to spiritualize the beatitude of Luke 6:20. From his point of view, to be poor in spirit is to be like those who, because they are materially poor, recognize their need and are disposed to receiving help.[12] In other words, "Interpreters can differ regarding their understanding of Jesus' solidarity with the poor and oppressed. However, no one can, without throwing out the evidence, deny that Jesus conceived his ministry as the initiation of a new era in which justice would be done to the poor."[13]

So it is in effect, among other reasons, because the synoptic gospels give evidence of the Galilean option of Jesus and of his special love for the insignificant, those from below, the disposable, the oppressed, the marginalized, and the poor of the earth. And the apostolic church followed in the same footsteps, understanding its vocation in history as following the Lord who "for your sakes . . . became poor, so that by his poverty you might become rich" (2 Cor 8:9). This means becoming incarnate in a concrete historical situation and taking up the cross each day, inserting ourselves into the path of discipleship as disciples faithful and obedient to the crucified and resurrected Jesus of Nazareth. We have no other option.

A CONTEXTUAL PERSPECTIVE

The existence of the poor and excluded is not mere statistical data or facts lacking specific social and political content. Nor is it a mere theological fashion or a reference case for theological reflection and for the practice of love for neighbor. Both things express concrete realities that constitute enormous challenges for the mission of evangelical churches situated in the two-thirds world. Faced with the scandal of abject poverty that millions of human beings find themselves in and the undeniable condition

11. Padilla, "Jesús y los Pobres," 152, my translation.

12. Ibid., 153.

13. Ibid., 155, my translation.

of social and political exclusion of millions of human beings of flesh and bone, the disciples of Jesus of Nazareth cannot remain unmoved or keep silent. The emphatic denunciation of the Old Testament prophets that shook the society of their time, the solidarity of Jesus of Nazareth with the poor and the oppressed, the practices of solidarity of the apostolic church and of the communities of disciples that were shaped as a consequence of the proclamation of the good news of the kingdom of God outside of the limits of Palestine, constitute sufficient spiritual fuel to forge concrete models of service to neighbor. The route is laid out and the models are outlined both in the Old and in the New Testament. But the disciples of the Teacher from Galilee must run the risk of being obedient to all of God's counsel in the distinct historical contexts that they are situated in to be friends of life, peacemakers, ambassadors of justice, living examples of solidarity with concrete human beings, builders of new human relations, and architects of a just and solidary society.

God is a friend of life. He is the God of life. The refined and subtle forms of assassinating millions of innocent people and of devaluing the human dignity of orphans, widows, and foreigners (immigrants) of today form part of the diabolical circle of death and violence, contrary to God's liberating purpose. According to the biblical teaching, real human beings have an unquestionable intrinsic value, a non-negotiable value that cannot be lowered or auctioned off according to the criteria of supply and demand. The life of a human being is much more valuable than the prejudices and the theological short-sightedness of the modern Pharisees, for whom the poor and excluded constitute mere objects of theological discussion or a good pretext for obtaining the material assistance of financial organizations and channels of international cooperation. Both the Old and the New Testament teach that God is concerned with, fights for, protects, and loses face for all those who the powerful of this world consider as disposable trash. God is concerned with the social sectors that those who hold the political and economic power marginalize, exclude, and condemn to the dung heap of history. The challenge is posed. Whoever risks themselves to follow the crucified and resurrected Jesus of Nazareth through the dusty roads of contemporary cities and villages, walking among two or more fires in extreme situations of death and violence "will perhaps discover that God has a 'preference for the poor' that outrages some good evangelicals."[14]

14. Escobar, "Plentitud de la Misión," 9, my translation.

The biblical perspective is explicit and decisive. God's special love for the defenseless, the weak, the insignificant, the "nobodies" and the "nothings" according to official discourse, challenges the Christian church to shake off its comfortable theological presuppositions and missionary guidelines, permitting that the God of life speak by the force of his Word, so that in the power of his Spirit, it proclaims with words and deeds the good news of the kingdom of God, that where the communion bread is dear, love is definitive: the table of the poor and the excluded. The Galilean option is a calling for today. Voluntary renunciation for the cause of Jesus, at the foot of the cross, summons us to a radical discipleship that has as one of its core components the call to spend ourselves on behalf of the poor and excluded, to be a counterculture or an alternative community within a society that worships success and the market as supreme values. Cross and resurrection, danger of death and hope, interweave and mutually fertilize the path of faithful and obedient discipleship to the crucified and resurrected Jesus. The God of life challenges us to follow him in the Galilees of our time. But he also challenges us to follow him in the contemporary Jerusalems, so that inserted in the circles of power and without renouncing our identity as disciples of Jesus of Nazareth, we might forge concrete models of commitment to our neighbors, particularly in selfless service to the poor and the excluded of our time.

Bibliography

Arrastía, Cecilio. *Itinerario de la Pasión: Meditaciones para la Semana Santa* [*Itinerary of the Passion: Meditations for Holy Week*]. 3rd ed. El Paso, TX: Casa Bautista de Publicaciones, 1985.

Barclay, William. *The Daily Study Bible: The Gospel of Luke.* Louisville: Westminster John Knox, 2001. First published in 1953 by Saint Andrew Press.

————. *Jesus Christ for Today.* Nashville: Discipleship Resources, 1980. First published in 1973 by The World Methodist Council.

Barton, S. C. "Child, Children." In *Dictionary of Jesus and the Gospels*, edited by Joel B. Green, Scot McKnight, and I. Howard Marshall, 100–104. Downers Grove, IL: InterVarsity, 1992.

Bock, Darrell L. *Luke.* The IVP New Testament Commentary Series, edited by Grant R. Osborne. Downers Grove, IL: InterVarsity, 1994.

Bonhoeffer, Dietrich. *The Cost of Discipleship.* Translated by R. H. Fuller with some revision by Irmgard Booth. 2nd ed. New York: Macmillan, 1963.

Bosch, David J. "Mission in Jesus' Way: A Perspective from Luke's Gospel." *Missionalia* 17 (1989) 3–21.

————. *Transforming Mission: Paradigm Shifts in Theology of Mission.* American Society of Missiology Series 16. Maryknoll, NY: Orbis, 1991.

Bruce, F. F. *The Message of the New Testament.* Grand Rapids: Eerdmans, 1973. First published in 1972 by Paternoster.

Calvin, John. *Institutes of the Christian Religion.* 2 vols. 7th ed. Translated by John Allen. Philadelphia: Presbyterian Board of Christian Education, 1949.

Cassidy, Richard J. *Jesus, Politics, Society: A Study of Luke's Gospel.* Maryknoll, NY: Orbis, 1978.

Cassidy, Richard J., and Philip J. Scharper, editors. *Political Issues in Luke-Acts.* Maryknoll, NY: Orbis, 1983.

Cole, R. Alan. *The Gospel According to Mark: An Introduction and Commentary.* 2nd ed. The Tyndale New Testament Commentaries, edited by Leon Morris. Grand Rapids: Eerdmans, 1989.

Conzelmann, Hans. *The Theology of St. Luke*. Translated by Geoffrey Buswell. New York: Harper & Row, 1960.

Costas, Orlando. "La Misión como Discipulado" [Mission as discipleship]. *Boletín Teológico* 6 (1982) 45–59.

Craddock, Fred B. *Luke*. Interpretation series, edited by James Luther Mays. Louisville: Westminster John Knox, 1990.

Cullman, Oscar. *Jesus and the Revolutionaries*. Translated by Gareth Putnam. New York: Harper & Row, 1970.

Cussianovich, Alejandro. *Religious Life and the Poor: Liberation Theology Perspectives*. Translated by John Drury. Maryknoll, NY: Orbis, 1979.

Douglas, J. D., et al. *New Bible Dictionary*. 3rd ed. Downers Grove, IL: InterVarsity, 1994.

Escobar, Samuel. "Avancemos en la Plentitud de la Misión: Un Comentário Latinamericano sobre la Misiología de San Pablo" [Let Us Advance in the Fullness of Mission: A Latin American Commentary on the Missiology of Saint Paul]. In *Misión en el Camino: Ensayos en Homenaje a Orlando E. Costas*, 1–16. Buenos Aires: Fraternidad Teológica Latinoamericana, 1992.

Escudero Freire, Carlos. *Devolver el Evangelio a los Pobres: A Propósito de Lucas 1–2* [*Returning the Gospel to the Poor: On the Subject of Luke 1–2*]. Biblioteca de Estudios Bíblicos 19. Salamanca, Spain: Ediciones Sígueme, 1977.

Esler, Philip Francis. *Community and Gospel in Luke-Acts: The Social and Political Motivations of Lucan Theology*. Society for New Testament Study Monograph Series 57, edited by G. N. Stanton. Cambridge: Cambridge University Press, 1987.

Feinberg, C. L. "Synagogue." In *New Bible Dictionary*, 3rd ed., edited by J. D. Douglas et al., 1142–43. Downers Grove, IL: InterVarsity, 1996.

Fitzmyer, Joseph A. *The Gospel According to Luke (I–IX)*. The Anchor Bible 28. New York: Doubleday, 1981.

Ford, J. Massyngbaerde. "Reconciliation and Forgiveness in Luke's Gospel." In *Political Issues in Luke-Acts*, edited by Richard J. Cassidy and Philip J. Scharper, 80–98. Maryknoll, NY: Orbis, 1983.

———. *My Enemy Is My Guest: Jesus and Violence in Luke*. Maryknoll, NY: Orbis, 1984.

France, R. T. *The Gospel According to Matthew: An Introduction and Commentary*. The Tyndale New Testament Commentaries, edited by Canon Leon Morris. Grand Rapids: Eerdmans, 1985.

Gnilka, Joachim. *El Evangelio Según San Marcos: Mc 1—8:26* [*The Gospel According to Mark: Mark 1—8:26*]. Vol. I. Biblioteca de Estudios Bíblicos 55. Salamanca, Spain: Sígueme, 1986.

———. *El Evangelio Según San Marcos: Mc 8:27—16:20* [*The Gospel According to Mark: Mark 8:27—16:20*]. Vol. II. Biblioteca de Estudios Bíblicos 56. Salamanca, Spain: Sígueme, 1986.

Gooding, David. *According to Luke: A New Exposition of the Third Gospel*. Grand Rapids: Eerdmans, 1987.

Green, Joel B. *The Gospel of Luke*. The New International Commentary on the New Testament, edited by Ned B. Stonehouse, F. F. Bruce, and Gordon D. Fee. Grand Rapids: Eerdmans, 1997.

Gutiérrez, Gustavo. *The God of Life*. Translated by Matthew J. O'Connell. Maryknoll, NY: Orbis, 1991.

———. "La Primera Declaración Messiánica" [The First Messianic Declaration]. *Páginas* 92 (1988) 6–9.

————. *A Theology of Liberation: History, Politics, and Salvation*. 15th ed. Translated and edited by Sister Caridad Inda and John Eagleson. Maryknoll, NY: Orbis, 1988.

Hendriksen, William. *New Testament Commentary: Exposition of the Gospel According to Mark*. Grand Rapids: Baker, 1975.

————. *New Testament Commentary: Exposition of the Gospel According to Luke*. Grand Rapids: Baker, 1978.

Hertig, Paul. "The Galilee Theme in Matthew: Transforming Mission through Marginality." *Missiology* 25.2 (1997) 155–63.

————. "The Jubilee Mission of Jesus in the Gospel of Luke: Reversals of Fortunes." *Missiology* 26.2 (1998) 167–79.

Jeremias, Joachim. *Abba y el Mensaje Central del Nuevo Testamento* [*Abba and the Central Message of the New Testament*]. 2nd ed. Biblioteca de Estudios Bíblicos 30. Salamanca, Spain: Sígueme, 1983.

————. *The Parables of Jesus*. 2nd ed. New York: Scribner's, 1972.

Kane, J. P. "Capernaum." In *New Bible Dictionary*, 3rd ed, edited by J. D. Douglas et al., 175–76. Downers Grove, IL: InterVarsity, 1996.

Laconi, Mauro. *San Lucas y Su Iglesia* [*Saint Luke and His Church*]. Translated by José Antonio Jáuregui. Estella, Spain: Verbo Divino, 1987.

Mackay, John A. ". . . *Mas Yo Os Digo*" [". . . *But I say unto you*"]. 2nd ed. Mexico City: Casa Unida, 1964.

————. *A Preface to Christian Theology*. New York: Macmillan, 1943.

Marshall, I. Howard. "Luke." In *The New Bible Commentary: Revised*, 3rd ed., edited by D. Guthrie, J. A. Motyer, A. M. Stibbs, and D. J. Wiseman, 887–925. Grand Rapids: Eerdmans, 1970.

————. *Luke: Historian and Theologian*. Grand Rapids: Zondervan, 1971.

————. "Luke, Gospel of." In *New Bible Dictionary*, 3rd ed., edited by J. D. Douglas et al., 704–6. Downers Grove, IL: InterVarsity, 1996.

Míguez Bonino, José. *Poder del Evangelio y Poder Político: La Participación de los Evangélicos en la Vida Política en América Latina* [*Power of the Gospel and Political Power: The Participation of Evangelicals in the Political Life of Latin America*]. Colección Fraternidad Teológica Latinoamerica 4, edited by C. René Padilla. Bueno Aires: Kairos, 1999.

Moltmann, Jürgen. *The Experiment Hope*. Translated by M. Douglas Meeks. Philadelphia: Fortress, 1975.

Morris, Leon. *The Gospel According to Luke: An Introduction and Commentary*. The Tyndale New Testament Commentaries, edited by Leon Morris. Grand Rapids: Eerdmans, 2002.

————. *The Gospel According to Matthew*. Grand Rapids: Eerdmans, 1992.

Moule, C. F. D. *The Gospel According to Mark*. Cambridge: Cambridge University Press, 1965.

O'Toole, Robert F. "Luke's Position on Politics and Society in Luke-Acts." In *Political Issues in Luke-Acts*, edited by Richard J. Cassidy and Philip J. Scharper, 1–17. Maryknoll, NY: Orbis, 1983.

Padilla, C. René. "El Evangelio de los Pobres" [The Gospel of the Poor]. *Certeza* 60 (1975) 96–97.

————. "Jesús y los Pobres" [Jesus and the Poor]. *Certeza* 77 (1980) 151–56.

————. *Mission between the Times: Essays on the Kingdom*. Grand Rapids: Eerdmans, 1985.

————. *La Opción Galilea* [*The Galilean Option*]. Unpublished manuscript.

————. "Ser Prójimo" [Being a Neighbor]. *Certeza* 69 (1978) 147–50.

Padilla, C. René, editor. *Bases Bíblicas de la Misión: Perspectivas Latinoamericanas* [*Biblical Foundations for Mission: Latin American Perspectives*]. Grand Rapids: Eerdmans, 1998.

Perkins, John. *With Justice for All*. Ventura, CA: Regal, 1982.

Péry, A. "Poor." In *A Companion to the Bible*, edited by Jean-Jacques von Allmen, 327–28. New York: Oxford University Press, 1958.

Rigaux, Beda. *Para una Historia de Jesús: El Testimonio del Evangelio de Lucas* [*A Story of Jesus: The Testimony of the Gospel of Luke*]. Bilbao: Descleé de Brouwer, 1973.

Rivera Pagán, Luis. *Fe y Cultura en Puerto Rico* [*Faith and Culture in Puerto Rico*]. San Juan, PR: 2002.

Roux, H. "Kingdom." In *A Companion to the Bible*, edited by Jean-Jacques von Allmen, 217–21. New York: Oxford University Press, 1958.

Ryan, Rosalie. "The Women from Galilee and Discipleship in Luke." *Biblical Theology Bulletin* 15.2 (1985) 56–59.

Saracco, Norberto. "The Liberating Options of Jesus." In *Sharing Jesus in the Two Thirds World: Evangelical Christologies from the Contexts of Poverty, Powerlessness, and Religious Pluralism*, edited by Vinay Samuel and Chris Sugden, 33–41. Grand Rapids: Eerdmans, 1984.

Schottroff, Luise, and Wolfgang Stegemann. *Jesus and the Hope of the Poor*. Translated by Matthew J. O'Connell. Maryknoll, NY: Orbis, 1986.

Senior, Donald, and Carroll Stuhlmueller. *The Biblical Foundations for Mission*. Maryknoll, NY: Orbis, 1983.

Stott, John R. W. *The Message of Ephesians: God's New Society*. The Bible Speaks Today, edited by John R. W. Stott. Downers Grove, IL: InterVarsity, 1986.

———. *The Message of the Sermon on the Mount (Matthew 5–7): Christian Counter-Culture*. The Bible Speaks Today, edited by John R. W. Stott. Downers Grove, IL: InterVarsity, 1985.

Strange, W. A. *Children in the Early Church: Children in the Ancient World, the New Testament and the Early Church*. Carlisle, England: Paternoster, 1996.

Swartley, William M. "Politics or Peace (*Eirēnē*) in Luke's Gospel." In *Political Issues in Luke-Acts*, edited by Richard J. Cassidy and Philip S. Scharper, 18–37. Maryknoll, NY: Orbis, 1983.

Wenham, David. "How Jesus Understood the Last Supper: A Parable in Action." *Themelios* 20.2 (1995) 11–16.

———. *The Parables of Jesus*. The Jesus Library, edited by Michael Green. Downers Grove, IL: InterVarsity, 1989.

Yoder, John Howard. *The Politics of Jesus: Vicit Agnus Noster*. Grand Rapids: Eerdmans, 1972.

Zuck, Roy B. *Precious in His Sight: Childhood and Children in the Bible*. Grand Rapids: Baker, 1996.

Lightning Source UK Ltd.
Milton Keynes UK
UKOW030622280613

212925UK00010B/526/P